3.5⁰

THE
FORGOTTEN
LANGUAGE

BOOKS BY *Erich Fromm*

Erich Fromm

THE
FORGOTTEN
LANGUAGE

AN INTRODUCTION TO THE
UNDERSTANDING OF
DREAMS, FAIRY TALES
AND MYTHS

Grove Press, Inc.   New York

First Evergreen Edition 1957

Twenty-fourth Printing

DISTRIBUTED BY RANDOM HOUSE, INC., NEW YORK

Library of Congress Catalog Card No. 57-5156

GROVE PRESS, INC., 53 EAST 11TH STREET,
NEW YORK, NEW YORK 10003

Foreword

THIS BOOK IS BASED ON LECTURES WHICH I GAVE, AS AN
introductory course, to the postgraduate students in
training at the William A. White Institute of Psychiatry
and to undergraduate students at Bennington College.
It is addressed to a similar audience, to the student of
psychiatry and psychology and to the interested layman. As the subtitle indicates, this book is an *introduction* into the understanding of symbolic language;
for this reason it does not deal with many of the more
complicated problems in this field, the discussion of
which would have been incompatible with the purpose
of an introduction. I have thus, for instance, discussed
Freud's theory only on the level of his "Interpretation
of Dreams" and not in the light of the more difficult
concepts he developed in his later writings; nor have
I attempted to discuss those aspects of symbolic language which, although necessary for the full understanding of the problems involved, presuppose the more
general information which these pages try to convey.

I intend to deal with these problems in a second volume later on.

The term, an introduction to the *understanding* of dreams, etc., was chosen intentionally instead of using the more conventional term *interpretation*. If, as I shall try to show in the following pages, symbolic language is a language in its own right, in fact, the only universal language the human race ever developed, then the problem is indeed one of understanding it rather than of interpreting as if one dealt with an artificially manufactured secret code. I believe that such understanding is important for every person who wants to be in touch with himself, and not only for the psychotherapist who wants to cure mental disturbances; hence I believe that the understanding of symbolic language should be taught in our high schools and colleges just as other "foreign languages" are part of their curriculum. One of the aims of this book is to contribute to the realization of this idea.

I am indebted to Dr. Edward S. Tauber for reading the manuscript and for his constructive criticisms and suggestions.

I wish to thank Dr. Ruth N. Anshen, editor of *The Family, Its Function and Destiny*, and Harper Brothers for permission to make use, in the present volume, of my article "The Oedipus Myth and the Oedipus Complex." Furthermore, I wish to thank the following publishers for the privilege of using extensive passages from their publications: Random House, New York, excerpts from the Modern Library Edition of Plato. *The Republic*, trans. by B. Jowett, "Oedipus at Colonus" and "Antigone" trans. by R. C. Jebb from *The Complete Greek Drama, The Basic Writings of Sigmund Freud*, trans. and edited by A. A. Brill, and excerpts from Ralph L. Wood's *The World of Dreams;* Allen & Unwin, London, for excerpts from *The Interpretation of Dreams* by Sigmund Freud; Burns, Oates & Washbourne, Ltd., London, and Benziger Brothers, New York, for an excerpt from *Summa Theologica* by Thomas Aquinas, translated by the Fathers of the English Dominican Province; The Macmillan Company, New York, excerpt from Kant, *The Dreams of a Spirit Seer,* trans. by E. F. Goerwitz; Houghton Mifflin Company, Boston, excerpts from Ralph Waldo Emerson, *Lectures and Biographical Sketches;* Classics Club, W. J. Black, New York, excerpts from Plato, *Phaedo,* trans. by B. Jowett; Oxford Clarendon Press, excerpts from *The Works of Aristotle,* trans. under the editorship of W. D. Ross; Harvard University Press, Cambridge, excerpts from Lucretius, *De Rerum Natura,* trans. by W. H. D. Rouse; Yale University Press, New Haven, excerpts from C. J. Jung, *Psychology and Religion;* B. W. Huebsch, excerpts from Henri Bergson, *Dreams,* trans. by E. E. Slosson; Alfred A. Knopf, New York, excerpts from *The Trial* by Franz Kafka, trans. by E. I. Muir.

Erich Fromm

1951

Contents

A dream which is not understood is like a letter which is not opened.

—TALMUD

Sleep takes off the costume of circumstance, arms us with terrible freedom, so that every will rushes to a deed. A skillful man reads his dreams for his self-knowledge; yet not the details but the quality.

—EMERSON

nobody wonders about anything anymore.

I

Introduction

IF IT IS TRUE THAT THE ABILITY TO BE PUZZLED IS THE beginning of wisdom, then this truth is a sad commentary on the wisdom of modern man. Whatever the merits of our high degree of literary and universal education, we have lost the gift for being puzzled. Everything is supposed to be known—if not to ourselves then to some specialist whose business it is to know what we do not know. In fact, to be puzzled is embarrassing, a sign of intellectual inferiority. Even children are rarely surprised, or at least they try not to show that they are; and as we grow older we gradually lose the ability to be surprised. To have the right answers seems all-important; to ask the right questions is considered insignificant by comparison.

This attitude is perhaps one reason why one of the most puzzling phenomena in our lives, our dreams, gives so little cause for wonder and for raising questions. We all dream; we do not understand our dreams, yet we act as if nothing strange goes on in our sleep minds, strange at least by comparison with the logical, purposeful doings of our minds when we are awake.

When we are awake, we are active, rational be-

3

ings, eager to make an effort to get what we want and prepared to defend ourselves against attack. We act and we observe; we see things outside, perhaps not as they are, but at least in such a manner that we can use and manipulate them. But we are also rather unimaginative, and rarely—except as children or if we are poets—does our imagination go beyond duplicating the stories and plots that are part of our actual experience. We are effective but somewhat dull. We call the field of our daytime observation "reality" and are proud of our "realism" and our cleverness in manipulating it.

When we are asleep, we awake to another form of existence. We dream. We invent stories which never happened and sometimes for which there is not even any precedent in reality. Sometimes we are the hero, sometimes the villain; sometimes we see the most beautiful scenes and are happy; often we are thrown into extreme terror. But whatever the role we play in the dream *we* are the author, it is *our* dream, *we* have invented the plot.

Most of our dreams have one characteristic in common: they do not follow the laws of logic that govern our waking thought. The categories of space and time are neglected. People who are dead, we see alive; events which we watch in the present, occurred many years ago. We dream of two events as occurring simultaneously when in reality they could not possibly occur at the same time. We pay just as little attention to the laws of space. It is simple for us to move to a distant place in an instant, to be in two places at once, to fuse two persons into one, or to have one person suddenly be changed into another. Indeed, in our dreams we are the creators of a world where time and space, which limit all the activities of our body, have no power.

Another odd thing about our dreams is that we think of events and persons we have not thought of for years, and whom, in the waking state, we would never have remembered. Suddenly they appear in the dream as acquaintances whom we had thought of many times. In our sleeping life, we seem to tap the vast store of experience and memory which in the daytime we do not know exists.

Yet, despite all these strange qualities, our dreams are real to us while we are dreaming; as real as any experience we have in our waking life. There is no "as if" in the dream. The dream is present, real experience, so much so, indeed, that it suggests two questions: What is reality? How do we know that what we dream is unreal and what we experience in our waking life is real? A Chinese poet has expressed this aptly: "I dreamt last night that I was a butterfly and now I don't know whether I am a man who dreamt he was a butterfly, or perhaps a butterfly who dreams now that he is a man."

All these exciting, vivid experiences of the night not only disappear when we wake up, but we have the greatest difficulty trying to remember them. Most of them we simply forget, so completely that we do not even remember having lived in this other world. Some we faintly remember at the moment of waking, and the next second they are beyond recall. A few we do remember, and these are the ones we speak of when we say, "I had a dream." It is as if friendly, or unfriendly, spirits had visited us and at the break of day had suddenly disappeared; we hardly remember that they had been there and how intensely we had been occupied with them.

Perhaps more puzzling than all the factors already mentioned is the similarity of the products of our creativeness during sleep with the oldest creations of man —the myths.

Actually, we are not too much puzzled by myths. If they are made respectable as part of our religion, we give them a conventional and superficial acknowledgment as part of a venerable tradition; if they do not carry such traditional authority, they are taken for the childish expression of the thoughts of man before he was enlightened by science. At any rate, whether ignored, despised, or respected, myths are felt to belong to a world completely alien to our own thinking. Yet the fact remains that many of our dreams are, in both style and content, similar to myths, and we who find them strange and remote when we are awake have the ability to create these mythlike productions when we are asleep.

In the myth, too, dramatic events happen which are impossible in a world governed by the laws of time and space: the hero leaves his home and country to save the world, or he flees from his mission and lives in the belly of a big fish; he dies and is reborn; the mythical bird is burned and emerges from the ashes more beautiful than before.

Of course, different peoples created different myths just as different people dream different dreams. But in spite of all these differences, all myths and all dreams have one thing in common, they are all "written" in the same language, *symbolic language*.

The myths of the Babylonians, Indians, Egyptians, Hebrews, Greeks are written in the same language as those of the Ashantis or the Trukese. The dreams of someone living today in New York or in Paris are the same as the dreams reported from people living some thousand years ago in Athens or in Jerusalem. The dreams of ancient and modern man are written in the same language as the myths whose authors lived in the dawn of history.

Symbolic language is a language in which inner experiences, feelings and thoughts are expressed as if they were sensory experiences, events in the outer world. It is a language which has a different logic from the conventional one we speak in the daytime, a logic in which not time and space are the ruling categories but intensity and association. It is the one universal language the human race has ever developed, the same for all cultures and throughout history. It is a language with its own grammar and syntax, as it were, a language one must understand if one is to understand the meaning of myths, fairy tales and dreams.

Yet this language has been forgotten by modern man. Not when he is asleep, but when he is awake. Is it important to understand this language also in our waking state?

For the people of the past, living in the great cultures of both East and West, there was no doubt as to the answer to this question. For them myths and dreams were among the most significant expressions of the mind, and failure to understand them would have amounted to illiteracy. It is only in the past few hundred years of Western culture that this attitude has changed. At best, myths were supposed to be naïve fabrications of the prescientific mind, created long before man had made his great discoveries about nature and had learned some of the secrets of its mastery.

Dreams fared even worse in the judgment of modern enlightenment. They were considered to be plain senseless, and unworthy of the attention of grown-up men, who were busy with such important matters as building machines and considered themselves "realistic" because they saw nothing but the reality of things they could conquer and manipulate; realists who have a special word for each type of automobile, but only the one word "love" to express the most varied kinds of affective experience.

Moreover, if all our dreams were pleasant phantasmagorias in which our hearts' wishes were fulfilled, we might feel friendlier toward them. But many of them leave us in an anxious mood; often they are nightmares from which we awake gratefully acknowledging that we only dreamed. Others, though not nightmares, are disturbing for other reasons. They do not fit the person we are sure we are during daytime. We dream of hating people whom we believe we are fond of, of loving someone whom we thought we had no interest in. We dream of being ambitious, when we are convinced of being modest; we dream of bowing down and submitting, when we are so proud of our independence. But worse than all this is the fact that we do not understand our dreams while we, the waking person, are sure we can understand anything if we put our minds to it. Rather than be confronted with such an overwhelming proof of the limitations of our understanding, we accuse the dreams of not making sense.

A profound change in the attitude toward myths and dreams has taken place in the past few decades. This change was greatly stimulated by Freud's work. After starting out with the restricted aim of helping the neurotic patient to understand the reasons for his illness, Freud proceeded to study the dream as a universal human phenomenon, the same in the sick and in the healthy person. He saw that dreams were essentially no different from myths and fairy tales and that to understand the language of the one was to understand the language of the others. And the work of anthropologists focused new attention on myths. They were collected and studied, and some few pioneers in this field, like J. J. Bachofen, succeeded in throwing new light on the prehistory of man.

But the study of myths and dreams is still in its infancy. It suffers from various limitations. One is a certain dogmatism and rigidity that has resulted from the claims of various psychoanalytic schools, each insisting that it has the only true understanding of symbolic language. Thus we lose sight of the many-sidedness of symbolic language and try to force it into the Procrustean bed of one, and only one, kind of meaning.

Another limitation is that interpretation of dreams is still considered legitimate only when employed by the psychiatrist in the treatment of neurotic patients. On the contrary, I believe that symbolic language is the one foreign language that each of us must learn. Its understanding brings us in touch with one of the most significant sources of wisdom, that of the myth, and it brings us in touch with the deeper layers of our own personalities. In fact, it helps us to understand a level of experience that is specifically human because it is that level which is common to all humanity, in content as well as in style.

The Talmud says, "Dreams which are not interpreted are like letters which have not been opened." Indeed, both dreams and myths are important communications from ourselves to ourselves. If we do not understand the language in which they are written, we miss a great deal of what we know and tell ourselves in those hours when we are not busy manipulating the outside world.

Dreams bring us in touch with our inner-selves.

II

The Nature of
Symbolic Language

LET US ASSUME YOU WANT TO TELL SOMEONE THE DIF-
ference between the taste of white wine and red wine.
This may seem quite simple to you. *You* know the difference very well; why should it not be easy to explain
it to someone else? Yet you find the greatest difficulty
putting this taste difference into words. And probably
you will end up by saying, "Now look here, I can't explain it to you. Just drink red wine and then white wine,
and you will know what the difference is." You have no
difficulty in finding words to explain the most complicated machine, and yet words seem to be futile to describe a simple taste experience.

Are we not confronted with the same difficulty
when we try to explain a feeling experience? Let us take
a mood in which you feel lost, deserted, where the
world looks gray, a little frightening though not really
dangerous. You want to describe this mood to a friend,
but again you find yourself groping for words and
eventually feel that nothing you have said is an adequate explanation of the many nuances of the mood.

The following night you have a dream. You see yourself in the outskirts of a city just before dawn, the streets are empty except for a milk wagon, the houses look poor, the surroundings are unfamiliar, you have no means of accustomed transportation to places familiar to you and where you feel you belong. When you wake up and remember the dream, it occurs to you that the feeling you had in that dream was exactly the feeling of lostness and grayness you tried to describe to your friend the day before. It is just one picture, whose visualization took less than a second. And yet this picture is a more vivid and precise description than you could have given by talking *about* it at length. The picture you see in the dream is a *symbol* of something you felt.

What is a symbol? A symbol is often defined as "something that stands for something else." This definition seems rather disappointing. It becomes more interesting, however, if we concern ourselves with those symbols which are sensory expressions of seeing, hearing, smelling, touching, standing for a "something else" which is an inner experience, a feeling or thought. A symbol of this kind is something outside ourselves; that which it symbolizes is something inside ourselves. Symbolic language is language in which we express inner experience as if it were a sensory experience, as if it were something we were doing or something that was done to us in the world of things. Symbolic language is language in which the world outside is a symbol of the world inside, a symbol for our souls and our minds.

If we define a symbol as "something which stands for something else," the crucial question is: *What is the specific connection between the symbol and that which it symbolizes?*

In answer to this question we can differentiate between three kinds of symbols: the *conventional,* the *accidental* and the *universal* symbol. As will become apparent presently, only the latter two kinds of symbols express inner experiences as if they were sensory experiences, and only they have the elements of symbolic language.

The *conventional* symbol is the best known of the three, since we employ it in everyday language. If we see the word "table" or hear the sound "table," the letters T-A-B-L-E stand for something else. They stand for the thing table that we see, touch and use. What is the connection between the *word* "table" and the *thing* "table"? Is there any inherent relationship between them? Obviously not. The thing table has nothing to do with the sound table, and the only reason the word symbolizes the thing is the convention of calling this particular thing by a particular name. We learn this connection as children by the repeated experience of hearing the word in reference to the thing until a lasting association is formed so that we don't have to think to find the right word.

There are some words, however, where the association is not only conventional. When we say "phooey," for instance, we make with our lips a movement of dispelling the air quickly. It is an expression of disgust in which our mouths participate. By this quick expulsion of air we imitate and thus express our intention to expel something, to get it out of our system. In this case, as in some others, the symbol has an inherent connection with the feeling it symbolizes. But even if we assume that originally many or even all words had their origins in some such inherent connection between symbol and the symbolized, most words no longer have this meaning for us when we learn a language.

Words are not the only illustration for conventional symbols, although they are the most frequent and best-known ones. Pictures also can be conventional symbols. A flag, for instance, may stand for a specific country, and yet there is no connection between the specific colors and the country for which they stand. They have been accepted as denoting that particular country, and we translate the visual impression of the flag into the concept of that country, again on conventional grounds. Some pictorial symbols are not entirely conventional; for example, the cross. The cross can be merely a conventional symbol of the Christian church and in that respect no different from a flag. But the specific content of the cross referring to Jesus' death or, beyond that, to the interpenetration of the material and spiritual planes, puts the connection between the symbol and what it symbolizes beyond the level of mere conventional symbols.

The very opposite to the conventional symbol is the *accidental* symbol, although they have one thing in common: there is no intrinsic relationship between the symbol and that which it symbolizes. Let us assume that someone has had a saddening experience in a certain city; when he hears the name of that city, he will easily connect the name with a mood of sadness, just as he would connect it with a mood of joy had his experience been a happy one. Quite obviously there is nothing in the nature of the city that is either sad or joyful. It is the individual experience connected with the city that makes it a symbol of a mood.

The same reaction could occur in connection with a house, a street, a certain dress, certain scenery, or anything once connected with a specific mood. We might find ourselves dreaming that we are in a certain city. In fact, there may be no particular mood connected with it in the dream; all we see is a street or even simply the name of the city. We ask ourselves why we happened to think of that city in our sleep and may discover that we had fallen asleep in a mood similar to the one symbolized by the city. The picture in the dream represents this mood, the city "stands for" the mood once experienced in it. Here the connection between the symbol and the experience symbolized is entirely accidental.

In contrast to the conventional symbol, the accidental symbol cannot be shared by anyone else except as we relate the events connected with the symbol. For this reason accidental symbols are rarely used in myths, fairy tales, or works of art written in symbolic language because they are not communicable unless the writer adds a lengthy comment to each symbol he uses. In dreams, however, accidental symbols are frequent, and later in this book I shall explain the method of understanding them.

The *universal* symbol is one in which there is an intrinsic relationship between the symbol and that which it represents. We have already given one example, that of the outskirts of the city. The sensory experience of a deserted, strange, poor environment has indeed a significant relationship to a mood of lostness and anxiety. True enough, if we have never been in the outskirts of a city we could not use that symbol, just as the word "table" would be meaningless had we never seen a table. This symbol is meaningful only to city dwellers and would be meaningless to people living in cultures that have no big cities. Many other universal symbols, however, are rooted in the experience of every human being. Take, for instance, the symbol of fire. We are fascinated by certain qualities of fire in a fireplace. First of all, by its aliveness. It changes continuously, it moves all the time, and yet there is constancy in it. It remains the same without being the same. It gives the impression of power, of energy, of grace and lightness. It is as if it were dancing and had an inexhaustible source of energy. When we use fire as a symbol, we describe the inner experience characterized by the same elements which we notice in the sensory experience of fire; the mood of energy, lightness, movement, grace, gaiety— sometimes one, sometimes another of these elements being predominant in the feeling.

Similar in some ways and different in others is the symbol of water—of the ocean or of the stream. Here, too, we find the blending of change and permanence, of constant movement and yet of permanence. We also feel the quality of aliveness, continuity and energy. But there is a difference; where fire is adventurous, quick, exciting, water is quiet, slow and steady. Fire has an element of surprise; water an element of predictability. Water symbolizes the mood of aliveness, too, but one which is "heavier," "slower," and more comforting than exciting.

That a phenomenon of the physical world can be the adequate expression of an inner experience, that the world of things can be a symbol of the world of the mind, is not surprising. We all know that our bodies express our minds. Blood rushes to our heads when we are furious, it rushes away from them when we are afraid; our hearts beat more quickly when we are angry, and the whole body has a different tonus if we are happy from the one it has when we are sad. We express our moods by our facial expressions and our attitudes and feelings by movements and gestures so precise that others recognize them more accurately from our gestures than from our words. Indeed, the body is a symbol—and not an allegory—of the mind. Deeply and genuinely felt emotion, and even any genuinely felt thought, is expressed in our whole organism. In the case of the universal symbol, we find the same connection between mental and physical experience. Certain physical phenomena suggest by their very nature certain emotional and mental experiences, and we express emotional experiences in the language of physical experiences, that is to say, symbolically.

The universal symbol is the only one in which the relationship between the symbol and that which is symbolized is not coincidental but intrinsic. It is rooted in the experience of the affinity between an emotion or thought, on the one hand, and a sensory experience, on the other. It can be called universal because it is shared by all men, in contrast not only to the accidental symbol, which is by its very nature entirely personal, but also to the conventional symbol, which is restricted to a group of people sharing the same convention. The universal symbol is rooted in the properties of our body, our senses, and our mind, which are common to all men and, therefore, not restricted to individuals or to specific groups. Indeed, the language of the universal symbol is the one common tongue developed by the human race, a language which it forgot before it succeeded in developing a universal conventional language.

There is no need to speak of a racial inheritance in order to explain the universal character of symbols. Every human being who shares the essential features of bodily and mental equipment with the rest of mankind is capable of speaking and understanding the symbolic language that is based upon these common properties. Just as we do not need to learn to cry when we are sad or to get red in the face when we are angry, and just as these reactions are not restricted to any particular race or group of people, symbolic language does not have to be learned and is not restricted to any segment of the human race. Evidence for this is to be found in the fact that symbolic language as it is employed in myths and dreams is found in all cultures in so-called primitive as well as such highly developed cultures as Egypt and Greece. Furthermore, the symbols used in these various cultures are strikingly similar since they all go back to the basic sensory as well as emotional experiences shared by men of all cultures. Added evidence is to be found in recent experiments in which people who had no knowledge of the theory of dream interpretation were able, under hypnosis, to interpret the symbolism of their dreams without any difficulty. After emerging from the hypnotic state and being asked to interpret the same dreams, they were puzzled and said, "Well, there is no meaning to them—it is just nonsense."

The foregoing statement needs qualification, however. Some symbols differ in meaning according to the difference in their realistic significance in various cultures. For instance, the function and consequently the meaning of the sun is different in northern countries and in tropical countries. In northern countries, where water is plentiful, all growth depends on sufficient sunshine. The sun is the warm, life-giving, protecting, loving power. In the Near East, where the heat of the sun is much more powerful, the sun is a dangerous and even threatening power from which man must protect himself, while water is felt to be the source of all life and the main condition for growth. We may speak of dialects of universal symbolic language, which are determined by those differences in natural conditions which cause certain symbols to have a different meaning in different regions of the earth.

Quite different from these "symbolic dialects" is the fact that many symbols have more than one meaning in accordance with different kinds of experiences which can be connected with one and the same natural phenomenon. Let us take up the symbol of fire again. If we watch fire in the fireplace, which is a source of pleasure and comfort, it is expressive of a mood of aliveness, warmth, and pleasure. But if we see a building or forest on fire, it conveys to us an experience of threat or terror, of the powerlessness of man against the elements of nature. Fire, then, can be the symbolic representation of inner aliveness and happiness as well as of fear, powerlessness, or of one's own destructive tendencies. The same holds true of the symbol water. Water can be a most destructive force when it is whipped up by a storm or when a swollen river floods its banks. Therefore, it can be the symbolic expression of horror and chaos as well as of comfort and peace.

Another illustration of the same principle is a symbol of a valley. The valley enclosed between mountains can arouse in us the feeling of security and comfort, of protection against all dangers from the outside. But the protecting mountains can also mean isolating walls which do not permit us to get out of the valley and thus the valley can become a symbol of imprisonment. The particular meaning of the symbol in any given place can only be determined from the whole context in which the symbol appears, and in terms of the predominant experiences of the person using the symbol. We shall return to this question in our discussion of dream symbolism.

A good illustration of the function of the universal symbol is a story, written in symbolic language, which is known to almost everyone in Western culture: the Book of Jonah. Jonah has heard God's voice telling him to go to Nineveh and preach to its inhabitants to give up their evil ways lest they be destroyed. Jonah cannot help hearing God's voice and that is why he is a prophet. But he is an unwilling prophet, who, though knowing what he should do, tries to run away from the command of God (or, as we may say, the voice of his conscience). He is a man who does not care for other human beings. He is a man with a strong sense of law and order, but without love.[1]

How does the story express the inner processes in Jonah?

We are told that Jonah went down to Joppa and found a ship which should bring him to Tarshish. In mid-ocean a storm rises and, while everyone else is excited and afraid, Jonah goes into the ship's belly and falls into a deep sleep. The sailors, believing that God must have sent the storm because someone on the ship is to be punished, wake Jonah, who had told them he was trying to flee from God's command. He tells them to take him and cast him forth into the sea and that the sea would then become calm. The sailors (betraying a remarkable sense of humanity by first trying everything else before following his advice) eventually take Jonah and cast him into the sea, which immediately stops raging. Jonah is swallowed by a big fish and stays in the fish's belly three days and three nights. He prays to God to free him from this prison. God makes the fish vomit out Jonah unto the dry land and Jonah goes to Nineveh, fulfills God's command, and thus saves the inhabitants of the city.

[1] Cf. the discussion of Jonah in E. Fromm's *Man for Himself*, (New York, Rinehart & Co., 1947), where the story is discussed from the point of view of the meaning of love.

The story is told as if these events had actually happened. However, it is written in symbolic language and all the realistic events described are symbols for the inner experiences of the hero. We find a sequence of symbols which follow one another: going into the ship, going into the ship's belly, falling asleep, being in the ocean, and being in the fish's belly. All these symbols stand for the same inner experience: for a condition of being protected and isolated, of safe withdrawal from communication with other human beings. They represent what could be represented in another symbol, the fetus in the mother's womb. Different as the ship's belly, deep sleep, the ocean, and a fish's belly are realistically, they are expressive of the same inner experience, of the blending between protection and isolation.

In the manifest story events happen in space and time: *first*, going into the ship's belly; *then*, falling asleep; *then*, being thrown into the ocean; *then*, being swallowed by the fish. One thing happens after the other and, although some events are obviously unrealistic, the story has its own logical consistency in terms of time and space. But if we understand that the writer did not intend to tell us the story of external events, but of the inner experience of a man torn between his conscience and his wish to escape from his inner voice, it becomes clear that his various actions following one after the other express the same mood in him; and that *sequence in time* is expressive of a *growing intensity* of the same feeling. In his attempt to escape from his obligation to his fellow men Jonah isolates himself more and more until, in the belly of the fish, the protective element has so given way to the imprisoning element that he can stand it no longer and is forced to pray to God to be released from where he had put himself. (This is a mechanism which we find so characteristic of neurosis. An attitude is assumed as a defense against a danger, but then it grows far beyond its original defense function and becomes a neurotic symptom from which the person tries to be relieved.) Thus Jonah's escape into protective isolation ends in the terror of being imprisoned, and he takes up his life at the point where he had tried to escape.

There is another difference between the logic of the manifest and of the latent story. In the manifest story the logical connection is one of causality of external events. Jonah wants to go overseas *because* he wants to flee from God, he falls asleep *because* he is tired, he is thrown overboard *because* he is supposed to be the reason for the storm, and he is swallowed by the fish *because* there are man-eating fish in the ocean. One event occurs because of a previous event. (The last part of the story is unrealistic but not illogical.) But in the latent story the logic is different. The various events are related to each other by their association with the same inner experience. What appears to be a causal sequence of external events stands for a connection of experiences linked with each other by their association in terms of inner events. This is as logical as the manifest story—but it is a logic of a different kind. If we turn now to an examination of the nature of the dream, the logic governing symbolic language will become more **transparent.**

III

The Nature of Dreams

THE VIEWS HELD ABOUT THE NATURE OF DREAMS DIFfered vastly throughout the centuries and through various cultures. But whether one believes that dreams are real experiences of our disembodied souls, which have left the body during sleep, or whether one holds that dreams are inspired by God, or by evil spirits, whether one sees in them the expression of our irrational passions or, in contrast, of our highest and most moral powers, one idea is not controversial: the view that all dreams are meaningful and significant. Meaningful, because they contain a message which can be understood if one has the key for its translation. Significant, because we do not dream of anything that is trifling, even though it may be expressed in a language which hides the significance of the dream message behind a trifling façade.

Only in recent centuries was there a radical departure from this view. Dream interpretation was relegated to the realm of superstitions, and the enlightened, educated person, layman or scientist, had no doubt that dreams were senseless and insignificant manifestations of our minds, at best mental reflexes of bodily sensations experienced during sleep.

24

It was Freud who, at the beginning of the twentieth century, reaffirmed the old concept: dreams are both meaningful and significant; we do not dream anything that is not an important expression of our inner lives and all dreams can be understood provided we have the key; the interpretation of dreams is the "via regia," the main avenue leading to the understanding of the unconscious and thereby to the most powerful motivating force in pathological as well as in normal behavior. Beyond this general statement about the nature of dreams Freud emphatically and somewhat rigidly reaffirmed one of the oldest theories: the dream is the fulfillment of irrational passions, repressed during our waking life.

Instead of presenting Freud's and the older theories of the dream at this point, I shall return to them in a later chapter and proceed now to discuss the nature of the dream as I have come to understand it, with the help of Freud's work and as the result of my own experience as a dreamer and as a dream interpreter.

In view of the fact that there is no expression of mental activity which does not appear in the dream, I believe that the only description of the nature of dreams that does not distort or narrow down the phenomenon is the broad one that *dreaming is a meaningful and significant expression of any kind of mental activity under the condition of sleep.*

Obviously this definition is too broad to be of much help for the understanding of the nature of dreams unless we can say something more definite about the "condition of sleep" and the particular effect of this condition on our mental activity. If we can find out what the specific effect of sleeping is on our mental activity, we may discover a good deal more about the nature of dreaming.

Physiologically, sleep is a condition of chemical regeneration of the organism; energy is restored while no action takes place and even sensory perception is almost entirely shut off. Psychologically, sleep suspends the main function characteristic of waking life: man's reacting toward reality by perception and action. This difference between the biological functions of waking and of sleeping is, in fact, a difference between two states of existence.

In order to appreciate the effect of sleep existence on our mental process, we must first consider a more general problem, that of the interdependence of the kind of activity we are engaged in and our thinking process. The way we think is largely determined by what we do and what we are interested in achieving. This does not mean that our thinking is distorted by our interest but simply that it differs according to it.

What is, for example, the attitude of different people toward a forest? A painter who has gone there to paint, the owner of the forest who wishes to evaluate his business prospects, an officer who is interested in the tactical problem of defending the area, a hiker who wants to enjoy himself—each of them will have an entirely different concept of the forest because a different aspect is significant to each one. The painter's experience will be one of form and color; the businessman's of size, number, and age of the trees, the officer's of visibility and protection; the hiker's of trails and motion. While they can all agree to the abstract statement that they stand at the edge of a forest, the different kinds of activity they are set to accomplish will determine their experience of "seeing a forest."

The difference between the biological and psychological functions of sleeping and waking is more fundamental than any difference between various kinds of activity, and accordingly the difference between the conceptual systems accompanying the two states is incomparably greater. In the waking state thoughts and feelings respond primarily to challenge—the task of mastering our environment, changing it, defending ourselves against it. Survival is the task of waking man; he is subject to the laws that govern reality. This means that he has to think in terms of time and space and that his thoughts are subject to the laws of time and space logic.

While we sleep we are not concerned with bending the outside world to our purposes. We are helpless, and sleep, therefore, has rightly been called the "brother of death." But we are also free, freer than when awake. We are free from the burden of work, from the task of attack or defense, from watching and mastering reality. We need not look at the outside world; we look at our inner world, are concerned exclusively with ourselves. When asleep we may be likened to a fetus or a corpse; we may also be likened to angels, who are not subject to the laws of "reality." In sleep the realm of necessity has given way to the realm of freedom in which "I am" is the only system to which thoughts and feelings refer.

Mental activity during sleep has a logic different from that of waking existence. Sleep experience need not pay any attention to qualities that matter only when one copes with reality. If I feel, for instance, that a person is a coward, I may dream that he changed from a man into a chicken. This change is logical in terms of what I feel about the person, illogical only in terms of my orientation to outside reality (in terms of what I could *do*, realistically, to or with the person). Sleep experience is not lacking in logic but is subject to different logical rules, which are entirely valid in that particular experiential state.

Sleep and waking life are the two poles of human existence. Waking life is taken up with the function of action, sleep is freed from it. Sleep is taken up with the function of self-experience. When we wake from our sleep, we move into the realm of action. We are then oriented in terms of this system, and our memory operates within it: we remember what can be recalled in space-time concepts. The sleep world has disappeared. Experiences we had in it—our dreams—are remembered with the greatest difficulty.[1] The situation has been represented symbolically in many a folk tale: at night ghosts and spirits, good and evil, occupy the scene, but when dawn arrives, they disappear, and nothing is left of all the intense experience.

From these considerations certain conclusions about the nature of the unconscious follow:

---

[1] Cf. to the problem of memory function in its relation to dream activity the very stimulating article by Dr. Ernest G. Schnachtel, "On Memory and Childhood Amnesia," *Psychiatry*, February, 1947.

It is neither Jung's mythical realm of racially inherited experience nor Freud's seat of irrational libidinal forces. It must be understood in terms of the principle: "What we think and feel is influenced by what we do."

Consciousness is the mental activity in our state of being preoccupied with external reality—with acting. The unconscious is the mental experience in a state of existence in which we have shut off communications with the outer world, are no longer preoccupied with action but with our self-experience. The unconscious is an experience related to a special mode of life—that of nonactivity; and the characteristics of the unconscious follow from the nature of this mode of existence. The qualities of consciousness, on the other hand, are determined by the nature of action and by the survival function of the waking state of existence.

The "unconscious" is the unconscious only in relation to the "normal" state of activity. When we speak of "unconscious" we really say only that an experience is alien to that frame of mind which exists while and as we act; it is then felt as a ghostlike, intrusive element, hard to get hold of and hard to remember. But the day world is as unconscious in our sleep experience as the night world is in our waking experience. The term "unconscious" is customarily used solely from the standpoint of day experience; and thus it fails to denote that both conscious and unconscious are only different states of mind referring to different states of existence.

It will be argued that in the waking state of existence, too, thinking and feeling are not entirely subject to the limitations of time and space; that our creative imagination permits us to think about past and future objects as if they were present, and of distant objects as if they were before our eyes; that our waking feeling is not dependent on the physical presence of the object nor on its co-existence in time; that, therefore, the absence of the space-time system is not characteristic of sleep existence in contradistinction to waking existence, but of thinking and feeling in contradistinction to acting. This welcome objection permits me to clarify an essential point in my argument.

We must differentiate between the *contents* of thought processes and the *logical categories* employed in thinking. While it is true that the contents of our waking thoughts are not subject to limitations of space and time, the categories of logical thinking are those of the space-time nature. I can, for instance, think of my father and state that his attitude in a certain situation is identical with mine. This statement is logically correct. On the other hand, if I state "I am my father," the statement is "illogical" because it is not conceived in reference to the physical world. The sentence is logical, however, in a purely experiential realm: it expresses the experience of identity with my father. Logical thought processes in the waking state are subject to categories which are rooted in a special form of existence—the one in which we relate ourselves to reality in terms of action. In my sleep existence, which is characterized by lack of even potential action, logical categories are employed which have reference only to my self-experience. The same holds true of feeling. When I feel, in the waking state, with regard to a person whom I have not seen for twenty years, I remain aware of the fact that the person is not present. If I dream about the person, my feeling deals with the person as if he or she were present. But to say "as if he were present" is to express the feeling in logical "waking life" concepts. In sleep existence there is no "as if"; the person *is* present.

In the foregoing pages the attempt has been made to describe the conditions of sleep and to draw from this description certain conclusions concerning the quality of dream activity. We must now proceed to study one specific element among the conditions of sleep which will prove to be of great significance to the understanding of dream processes. We have said that while we are asleep we are not occupied with managing outer reality. We do not perceive it and we do not influence it, nor are we subject to the influences of the outside world on us. From this it follows that the effect of this separation from reality depends on the quality of reality itself. If the influence from the outside world is essentially beneficial, the absence of this influence during sleep would tend to lower the value of our dream activity, so that it would be inferior to our mental activities during the daytime when we are exposed to the beneficial influence of outside reality.

But are we right in assuming that the influence of reality is exclusively a beneficial one? May it not be that it is also harmful and that, therefore, the absence of its influence tends to bring forth qualities superior to those we have when we are awake?

In speaking of the reality outside ourselves, reference is not made primarily to the world of nature. Nature as such is neither good nor bad. It may be helpful to us or dangerous, and the absence of our perception of it relieves us, indeed, from our task of trying to master it or of defending ourselves against it; but it does not make us either more stupid or wiser, better or worse. It is quite different with the man-made world around us, with the culture in which we live. Its effect upon us is quite ambiguous, although we are prone to assume that it is entirely to our benefit.

Indeed, the evidence that cultural influences are beneficial to us seems almost overwhelming. What differentiates us from the world of animals is our capacity to create culture. What differentiates the higher from the lower stages of human development is the variation in cultural level. The most elementary element of culture, language, is the precondition for any human achievement. Man has been rightly called a symbol-making animal, for without our capacity to speak, we could hardly be called human. But every other human function also depends on our contact with the outside world. We learn to think by observing others and by being taught by them. We develop our emotional, intellectual and artistic capacities under the influence of contact with the accumulation of knowledge and artistic achievement that created society. We learn to love and to care for others by contact with them, and we learn to curb impulses of hostility and egoism by love for others, or at least by fear of them.

Is, then, the man-made reality outside ourselves not the most significant factor for the development of the very best in us, and must we not expect that, when deprived of contact with the outside world, we regress temporarily to a primitive, animal-like, unreasonable state of mind? Much can be said in favor of such an assumption, and the view that such a regression is the essential feature of the state of sleep, and thus of dream activity, has been held by many students of dreaming from Plato to Freud. From this viewpoint dreams are expected to be expressions of the irrational, primitive strivings in us, and the fact that we forget our dreams so easily is amply explained by our being ashamed of those irrational and criminal impulses which we express when we were not under the control of society. Undoubtedly this interpretation of dreams is true, and we shall presently turn to it and give some illustrations. But the question is whether it is exclusively true or whether the negative elements in the influence of society do not account for the paradoxical fact that *we are not only less reasonable and less decent in our dreams but that we are also more intelligent, wiser, and capable of better judgment when we are asleep than when we are awake.*

Indeed, culture has not only a beneficial but also a detrimental influence on our intellectual and moral functions. Human beings are dependent on each other, they need each other. But human history up to now has been influenced by one fact: material production was not sufficient to satisfy the legitimate needs of all men. The table was set for only a few of the many who wanted to sit down and eat. Those who were stronger tried to secure places for themselves, which meant that they had to prevent others from getting seats. If they had loved their brothers as much as Buddha or the Prophets or Jesus postulated, they would have shared their bread rather than eat meat and drink wine without them. But, love being the highest and most difficult achievement of the human race, it is no slur on man that those who could sit at the table and enjoy the good things of life did not want to share, and therefore were compelled to seek power over those who threatened their privileges. This power was often the power of the conqueror, the physical power that forced the majority to be satisfied with their lot. But physical power was not always available or sufficient. One had to have power over the minds of people in order to make them refrain from using their fists. This control over mind and feeling was a necessary element in retaining the privileges of the few. In this process, however, the minds of the few became as distorted as the minds of the many. The guard who watches a prisoner becomes almost as much a prisoner as the prisoner himself. The "elite" who have to control those who are not "chosen" become the prisoners of their own restrictive tendencies. Thus the human mind, of both rulers and ruled, becomes deflected from its essential human purpose, which is to feel and to think humanly, to use and to develop the powers of reason and love that are inherent in man and without the full development of which he is crippled.

In this process of deflection and distortion man's character becomes distorted. Aims which are in contrast to the interests of his real human self become paramount. His powers of love are impoverished, and he is driven to want power over others. His inner security is lessened, and he is driven to seek compensation by passionate cravings for fame and prestige. He loses the sense of dignity and integrity and is forced to turn himself into a commodity, deriving his self-respect from his salability, from his success. All this makes for the fact that we learn not only what is true, but also what is false. That we hear not only what is good, but are constantly under the influence of ideas detrimental to life.

This holds true for a primitive tribe in which strict laws and customs influence the mind, but it is true also for modern society with its alleged freedom from rigid ritualism. In many ways the spread of literacy and of the media of mass communication has made the influence of cultural clichés as effective as it is in a small, highly restricted tribal culture. Modern man is exposed to an almost unceasing "noise," the noise of the radio, television, headlines, advertising, the movies, most of which do not enlighten our minds but stultify them. We are exposed to rationalizing lies which masquerade as truths, to plain nonsense which masquerades as common sense or as the higher wisdom of the specialist, of double talk, intellectual laziness, or dishonesty which speaks in the name of "honor" or "realism", as the case may be. We feel superior to the superstitions of former generations and so-called primitive cultures, and we are constantly hammered at by the very same kind of superstitious beliefs that set themselves up as the latest discoveries of science. Is it surprising, then, that to be awake is not exclusively a blessing but also a curse? Is it surprising that in a state of sleep, when we are alone with ourselves, when we can look into ourselves without being bothered by the noise and nonsense that surround us in the daytime, we are better able to feel and to think our truest and most valuable feelings and thoughts?

This, then, is the conclusion at which we arrive: the state of sleep has an ambiguous function. In it the lack of contact with culture makes for the appearance both of our worst *and* of our best; therefore, if we dream, we may be less intelligent, less wise, and less decent, but we may also be better and wiser than in our waking life.

Having arrived at this point, the difficult problem arises: how do we know whether a dream is to be understood as an expression of our best or of our worst? Is there any principle which can guide us in this attempt?

To answer this question we must leave the somewhat general level of our discussion and try to get further insight by discussing a number of concrete dream illustrations.

The following dream was reported by a man who had met a "very important person" the day before he had this dream. This person had the reputation of being wise and kind, and the dreamer had come to see him, impressed by what everyone said about the old man. He had left after an hour or so with a feeling that he had met a great and kind man.

> I see Mr. X [the very important person]; his face looks quite different from what it looked yesterday. I see a cruel mouth and a hard face. He is laughingly telling someone that he has just succeeded in cheating a poor widow out of her last few cents. I feel a sense of revulsion.

When asked to tell what occurred to him about this dream, the dreamer remarked that he could remember a fleeting feeling of disappointment when he walked into Mr. X's room and had a first glimpse of his face; this feeling, however, disappeared as soon as X started an engaging and friendly conversation.

How are we to understand this dream? Perhaps the dreamer is envious of Mr. X's fame and for this reason dislikes him? In that case the dream would be the expression of the irrational hate that the dreamer harbors without being aware of it. But in the case I am reporting here, it was different. At subsequent meetings, after our dreamer had become aware of his supicion through his dreams, he observed X carefully and discovered that there was in the man an element of ruthlessness which he had seen for the first time in his dream. His impression was corroborated by the few who dared to doubt the majority's opinion that X was such a kind man. It was corroborated by some facts in X's life which were by no means so crude as that in the dream, but which nevertheless were expressive of a similar spirit.

What we see, then, is that the dreamer's insight into the character of X was much more astute in his sleep than in his waking life. The "noise" of public opinion, which insisted that X was a wonderful man, prevented him from becoming aware of his critical feeling toward X when he saw him. It was only later, after he had this dream, that he could remember the split second of distrust and doubt he had felt. In his dream, when he was protected from this "noise" and in a position to be alone with himself and his impressions and feelings, he could make a judgment which was more accurate and true than his waking-state judgment.

In this, as in every other dream, we can decide whether the dream is expressive of irrational passion or of reason only if we consider the person of the dreamer, the mood he was in when he fell asleep, and whatever data we have on the reality aspect of the situation he has dreamed about. In this case our interpretation is corroborated by a number of factors. The dreamer could remember the initial fleeting impression of dislike. He had no reason to and did not harbor any hostile feelings against X. The data of X's life and later observations confirmed the impression the dreamer had had in his sleep. If all these factors were lacking, our interpretation would be different. For instance, if he were prone to be jealous of famous people, could not find any evidence for the dream judgment about X, could not remember the feeling of disgust when he saw him first, then, of course, we would be prone to assume that this dream was not an expression of insight but an expression of irrational hate.

Insight is closely related to prediction. To predict means to infer the future course of events from the direction and intensity of the forces that we can see at work at present. Any thorough knowledge, not of the surface but of the forces operating underneath it, will lead to making predictions, and any valuable prediction must be based on such knowledge. No wonder we often predict developments and events which are later borne out by the facts. Quite regardless of the question of telepathy, many dreams in which the dreamer forecasts future events fall into the category of rational predictions as we just defined them. One of the oldest dreams of prediction was Joseph's:

> And Joseph dreamed a dream, and he told it his brethren; and they hated him yet the more. And he said unto them, Hear, I pray you, this dream which I have dreamed: for, behold, we were binding sheaves in the field, and, lo, my sheaf arose, and also stood upright; and, behold, your sheaves stood round about, and made obeisance to my sheaf. And his brethren said to him, Shalt thou indeed reign over us? Or shalt thou indeed have dominion over us? And they hated him yet the more for his dreams, and for his words.

> And he dreamed yet another dream, and told it his brethren, and said, Behold, I have dreamed a dream more; and, behold, the sun and the moon and the eleven stars made obeisance to me. And he told it to his father, and to his brethren: and his father rebuked him, and said unto him, What is this dream that thou hast dreamed? Shall I and thy mother and thy brethren indeed come to bow down our-

selves to thee to the earth? And his brethren envied him; but his father observed the saying.

This report in the Old Testament shows us a situation in which dreams were still understood immediately by the "layman," and one did not yet need the help of an expert dream interpreter to understand a comparatively simple dream. (That to understand a more difficult dream one needed an expert is shown in the story of Pharaoh's dreams; where, in fact, the court dream interpreters were not able to understand his dreams and Joseph had to be brought in.) The brothers understand immediately that the dream is an expression of Joseph's fantasy that one day he will become superior to his father as well as to his brothers and that they would stand in awe of him. Undoubtedly this dream is an expression of Joseph's ambition, without which he probably would not have reached the high position he attained. But it happens that this dream came true, that it was not only an expression of irrational ambition but at the same time a prediction of events which actually occurred. How could Joseph make such a prediction? His life history in the Biblical report shows that he was not only an ambitious man, but a man of unusual talent. In his dream he is more closely aware of his extraordinary gifts than he could be in his waking life, where he was impressed by the fact that he was younger and weaker than all his brothers. His dream is a blend of his passionate ambition and an insight into his gifts without which his dream could not have come true.

A prediction of a different kind occurs in the following dream: A, who has met B to discuss a future business association, was favorably impressed and decided that he would take B into his business as a partner. The night after the meeting he had this dream:

I see B sitting in our common office. He is going over the books and changing figures in them in order to cover the fact that he has embezzled large sums of money.

A wakes up and, being accustomed to paying some attention to dreams, is puzzled. Being convinced that dreams are always the expression of our irrational desires, he tells himself that this dream is an expression of his own hostility and competitiveness with other men, that this hostility and suspicion lead him to a fantasy that B is a thief. Having interpreted the dream in this fashion, he leans over backwards to rid himself of these irrational suspicions. After he started the business association with B, a number of incidents occurred which re-aroused A's suspicion. But recalling his dream and its interpretation, he was convinced that again he was under the influence of irrational suspicions and feelings of hostility and decided to pay no attention to those circumstances which had made him suspicious. After one year, however, he discovered that B had embezzled considerable sums of money and covered it by false entries in the books. His dream had come true almost literally.

The analysis of A's association showed that his dream expressed an insight into B which he had gained at the first meeting, but of which he had not been aware in his waking thought. Those many and complex observations which we make about other persons in a split second without being aware of our own thought processes had made A recognize that B was dishonest. But, since there was no "evidence" for this view and since B's manner made it difficult for A's conscious thinking to believe in B's dishonesty, he had repressed the thought completely, or rather the thought had not even registered with him while he was awake. In his dream, however, he had the clear awareness of his suspicion and had he listened to this self-communication he could have avoided a good deal of trouble. His conviction that dreams were always the expression of our irrational fantasies and desires made him misread the dream and even certain later factual observations.

A dream which expresses moral judgment is that of a writer who had been offered a job in which he would earn a great deal more money than in his present position, but where he would also be forced to write things he did not believe in and to violate his personal integrity. Nevertheless, the offer was so tempting as far as money and prestige were concerned that he was not sure that he could reject it. He went through all the typical rationalizations that most people in such a situation go through. He reasoned that, after all, he might see the situation too black and that the concessions he would have to make were of a minor nature. Furthermore, even if he could not write as he pleased, this condition would last only for a few years and then he would give up the job, and have so much money that he would be

entirely independent and free to do the work that was
meaningful to him. He thought of his friends and family relations and what he could do for them. In fact, he
sometimes presented the problem to himself in such a
way that to accept the job seemed his moral obligation,
while to refuse it would be an expression of a self-indul-
gent, egotistical attitude. Nevertheless, none of these
rationalizations really satisfied him; he continued
doubting and was not able to make up his mind until
one night he had the following dream:

> I was sitting in a car at the foot of a high
> mountain where a narrow and exceedingly
> steep road began which led to the top of the
> mountain. I was doubtful whether I should
> drive up, since the road seemed very danger-
> ous. But a man who stood near my car told
> me to drive up and not to be afraid. I listened
> to him and decided to follow his advice. I
> drove up, and the road got more and more
> dangerous. I could not stop, though, because
> there was no possibility of turning around.
> When I was near the top the motor stalled,
> the brakes would not work, the car rolled
> back and fell over a precipice! I woke up in
> terror.

One association must be reported for the full understanding of the dream. The dreamer said that the
man who had encouraged him to drive up the mountain road was a former friend, a painter, who had "sold
out," become a fashionable portrait painter and made
a lot of money, but who at the same time had ceased to

be creative. He knew that in spite of his success this friend was unhappy and suffered from the fact that he had betrayed himself. To understand the whole dream is not difficult. The steep mountain this man was to drive up is a symbolic expression of the successful career about which he has to make his choice. In his dream he knows that this path is dangerous. He is aware of the fact that if he accepts the offer he will do exactly the same thing his friend has done, something for which he had despised his friend and because of which he had broken off their friendship. In the dream he is aware that this decision can only lead to his destruction. In the dream picture the destruction is that of his physical self, symbolizing his intellectual and spiritual self that is in danger of being destroyed.

The dreamer in his sleep saw the ethical problem clearly and recognized that he had to choose between "success," on the one hand, and integrity and happiness, on the other. He recognized what his fate would be if he made the wrong decision. In his waking state he could not see the alternative clearly. He was so impressed by the "noise" that says that it is stupid not to accept the chance to have more money, power and prestige. He was so influenced by the voices that say it is childish and impractical to be "idealistic" that he was caught in the many rationalizations one uses to drown out the voice of one's conscience. This particular dreamer, being aware of the fact that we often know more in our dreams than in our waking state, was sufficiently startled by this dream that the fog in his mind lifted, he was able to see the alternative clearly and made the decision for his integrity and against the self-destructive temptation.

Not only do insight into our relation to others or theirs to us, value judgments and predictions occur in our dreams, but also intellectual operations superior to those in the waking state. This is not surprising, since penetrating thinking requires an amount of concentration which we are often deprived of in the waking state, while the state of sleep is conducive to it. The best-known example of this kind of dream is the one of the discoverer of the Benzine ring. He had been searching for the chemical formula for Benzine for quite some time, and one night the correct formula stood before his eyes in a dream. He was fortunate enough to remember it after he awoke. There are numerous examples of people who look for solutions of a problem in mathematics, engineering, philosophy, or of practical problems, and one night they dream the solution with perfect clarity.

Sometimes one finds exceedingly complicated intellectual considerations occurring in dreams. The following illustration is an example of such a dream process, although it entails at the same time a very personal element. The dreamer is an intelligent woman and this is her dream:

> I saw a cat and many mice. And I thought, I shall ask my husband tomorrow morning why one hundred mice are not stronger than one cat, and why they cannot overpower her. I know he will answer me that this is no different from the historical

problem that dictators can rule over millions of people and not be overthrown by them. I knew, however, that this was a trick question and that his answer was wrong.

The morning following this dream she told her husband the first part of her dream and asked him, "What does it mean that I dreamed that the one hundred mice could not defeat one cat?" He promptly gave the answer she had anticipated in her dream. Two days later she recited to her husband a little poem she had composed. The poem dealt with a black cat who found herself on snow-covered fields surrounded by hundreds of mice. The mice were all laughing at the cat because, being black, she could be seen so clearly against the snow, and the cat wished to be white in order to be less visible. One line of the poem said, "And now I understand what puzzled me last night."

In repeating this poem to her husband, she was not aware of any connection between the poem and the dream. He saw the connection and said, "Well, so your poem gives the answer to your dream. You identified yourself not, as I had thought, with the mice, but with the cat; and in your dream you were proud that even one hundred mice could not defeat you. But at the same time you express a feeling of humiliation that the weak mice toward whom you feel so superior could laugh at you if they could see you very clearly." (The dreamer loves cats and feels sympathy and affinity with them.)

IV

Freud and Jung

MY DEFINITION OF DREAMING AS ANY KIND OF MENTAL activity under the condition of sleep, while based upon Freud's theory of dreams, is in sharp contrast to it in many ways. My assumption is that dreams can be the expression both of the lowest and most irrational *and* of the highest and most valuable functions of our minds. Freud assumes that dreams are always necessarily the expression of the irrational part of our personality. I shall try to show later in this book that these three theories: the dream as an exclusively irrational production, as an exclusively rational production, or as being either of the two, are to be found in the history of dream interpretation far back in the past. In view of the fact that Freud's interpretation of dreams is the beginning, the best-known and the most significant contribution of modern science to dream interpretation, I shall begin with a description and discussion of Freud's interpretation before I proceed to present the history of these three theories before Freud.

Freud's dream interpretation is based on the same principle as that which underlies his whole psychological theory: the concept that we can have strivings and feelings and wishes which motivate our actions and yet of which we have no awareness. He called such strivings "unconscious," and by this he meant that not only are we not aware of them but also that a powerful "censor" protects us from becoming aware of them. For any number of reasons, the most important of which is fear of losing the approval of our parents and friends, we repress such strivings, the awareness of which would make us feel guilty or afraid of punishment. However, the repression of such strivings from our awareness does not mean that they cease to exist. In fact they continue to exist so vigorously that they find expression in numerous forms, but in such a way that we are unaware of their having entered through the back door, as it were. Our conscious system thinks that it has got rid of such undesirable feelings and wishes and is horrified at the idea that they could be within us; when they do return and show their presence, they are, therefore, distorted and disguised to such an extent that our conscious thinking fails to recognize them for what they are.

In this way Freud explained the neurotic symptom. He assumed that powerful strivings kept from becoming conscious by the "censor" find expression in the symptom, but in a disguised fashion so that we are aware only of the suffering caused by the symptom and not of the satisfaction of these irrational strivings. Thus Freud recognized for the first time the neurotic symptom as something determined by forces within ourselves, and as something meaningful if one had the key to its understanding.

One example will illustrate this point. A woman complains about a compulsion to wash her hands every time she has touched anything. Quite naturally this has become an exceedingly troublesome symptom since it disrupts all her activities and makes her utterly miserable. She does not know why she has to do it. All she can say is that she feels an unbearable anxiety if she tries not to do it. The very fact that she has to obey an impulse which has taken possession of her without her knowing why adds greatly to her misery. Analyzing her fantasies and free associations, one discovers that the patient is coping with an intense feeling of hostility. Actually the beginning of her symptom coincides with the fact that her husband has started a love affair with another woman and left her in an abrupt and cruel manner. She had always been dependent on her husband and never dared to criticize or contradict him. Even when her husband announced his intention to leave her she hardly said a word, no reproach, no accusation, no anger. But the symptom began to take possession of her at that time. Further analysis showed that the patient had had a cruel and dominating father, one she was afraid of and toward whom she had never dared show anger or reproach. Analysis also showed that her meekness and submissiveness did not indicate the absence of rage. On the contrary, underneath her manifest behavior, rage had accumulated; this rage found expression only in fantasies as, for instance, seeing her father die, murdered or crippled. Her wish for revenge and her hate grew stronger, and yet her fear and the demands of her conscience forced her to repress such wishes almost completely. Her husband's behavior toward her revived this pent-up rage and added fuel to it. But here, too, she could not express it or even feel it Had she been aware of her hostility, she would have felt like killing or at least hurting her husband, and the neurotic symptoms might never have developed. As it was, her hostility operated in her and yet she was not aware of it.

The woman's symptom was a reaction to this hostility. Unconsciously, touching things became acts of destruction, and she had to wash her hands in order to cleanse herself from the destructive act she had committed. It was as though she had blood on her hands and had to wash it off again and again. The wash compulsion was the reaction to a hostile impulse, an attempt to undo the crime she had committed, and yet she was aware only of her need to wash her hands, while there was no awareness of the reasons for doing so. The symptom, which seemed to be a senseless act, could thus be understood as a meaningful piece of behavior once one had penetrated to the unconscious sector of her personality where her seemingly nonsensical behavior was rooted. Washing her hands was a compromise which permitted her to live out, though unconsciously, her rage and yet to cleanse herself from the guilt by the washing ceremony.

The discovery of the understanding of unconscious processes led Freud to a discovery which shed light on normal behavior. It permitted him to explain an error like forgetting or a slip-of-the-tongue which had puzzled many observers and for which no explanation had yet been found. We are all familiar with the phenomenon of suddenly not being able to remember a name which we know quite well. While it is true that such forgetting may have any number of causes, Freud discovered that often the explanation was to be found in the fact that something in us did not want to think of the name because it was associated with fear, anger, or other similar emotion. And that our wish to disassociate ourselves from the painful aspect led us to forget the name associated with it. As Nietzsche once said, "My memory says I have done this, my pride says I could not have done it. My memory yields."

The motive for such slips is not necessarily a feeling of fear or guilt. If someone meets a person and instead of "How do you do" the word "Good-by" slips out of his mouth, he has given expression to his real feeling: he wished he could immediately leave the person he had just met, or that he hadn't met him at all. Conventional considerations make it impossible for him to give expression to this feeling and yet his dislike for this person has made itself manifest behind his back, as it were. It put into his mouth the very words that express his real feelings while consciously he tended to indicate his pleasure at meeting the person.

Dreams are another part of behavior which Freud understands as an expression of unconscious strivings. He assumes that, as in the neurotic symptom or the error, the dream gives expression to unconscious strivings which we do not permit ourselves to be aware of and thus keep away from awareness when we are in full control of our thought. These repressed ideas and feelings become alive and find expression during sleep, and we call them dreams.

A number of more specific assumptions follow from this general concept of dreaming:

The motivating forces of our dream life are our irrational desires. In our sleep there come to life impulses whose existence we do not want to or dare not recognize when we are awake. Irrational hate, ambition, jealousy, envy, and particularly incestuous or perverse sexual desires which we exclude from our consciousness find expression in our dreams. Freud assumes that we all carry within us such irrational desires, which we have repressed because of demands of society but which we cannot get rid of entirely. During sleep our conscious control is weakened, and these desires come to life and make themselves heard in our dreams.

Freud goes one step further. He connects the theory of dreams with the function of sleep. Now, sleep is a physiological necessity and our organism tends to secure it as best it can. If we felt those intense, irrational desires in our sleep, we would be disturbed by them and eventually wake up. Thus these desires would interfere with the biological necessity to remain asleep. What do we do, then, in order to preserve our sleep? We imagine that our desires have been fulfilled, and thus are left with the feeling of satisfaction rather than a disturbing frustration.

Freud thus comes to the assumption that the essence of dreams is the hallucinatory fulfillment of irrational wishes; their function is the preserving of sleep. This explanation is understood more easily in those instances where the desire is not irrational and where, therefore, the dream is not distorted, as is the case with the average dream, according to Freud. Assume that someone has eaten a very salty dish before going to sleep and feels intense thirst during the night. He may dream that he is in search of water, finds a well and drinks great quantities of its cool and pleasant water. Instead of waking from his sleep in order to satisfy his thirst, he gives himself hallucinatory satisfaction by the fantasy of drinking water and this permits him to continue with his sleep. We are all familiar with a similar kind of hallucinatory satisfaction when we are awakened by the alarm clock and at that very moment produce a dream in which we hear church bells ringing and think it is Sunday and we need not get up so early. In this instance, too, the dream has served the function of protecting our sleep. Freud assumes that these simple fulfillments of wishes which in themselves are not irrational are relatively rare with adults, although more frequent with children, and that on the whole our dreams are a fulfillment not of such rational desires, but of the irrational desires that are repressed during the daytime.

A second assumption Freud makes about the nature of dreams is that these irrational desires which are expressed as fulfilled in the dream are rooted in our childhood, that they once were alive when we were children, that they have continued an underground existence, and have come to life in our dreams. This view is based on Freud's general assumption of the irrationality of the child.

To him the child has many asocial impulses. Since

it lacks the physical strength and the knowledge to act on its impulses, it is harmless and no one needs to protect himself against its evil designs. But if one focuses on the quality of its strivings rather than on their results in practice, the young child is an asocial and amoral being. This holds true in the first place for its sexual impulses. According to Freud, all those sexual strivings which, when they appear in the adult, are called perversions are part of the normal sexual development of the child. In the infant the sexual energy (libido) centers around the mouth, later it is connected with defecation, and eventually it centers around the genitals. The young child has intense sadistic and masochistic strivings. It is an exhibitionist and also a little "peeping Tom." It is not capable of loving anyone but is narcissistic, loving only itself to the exclusion of anyone else. It is intensely jealous and filled with destructive impulses against its rivals. The sexual life of the little boy and the little girl is dominated by incestuous strivings. They have a strong sexual attachment to the parent of the opposite sex and feel jealous of the parent of the same sex and hate him or her. Only the fear of retribution from the hated rival makes the child suppress these incestuous wishes. By identifying himself with the commands and prohibitions of the father, the little boy overcomes his hate against him and replaces it with the wish to be like him. The development of conscience is the result of the "Oedipus complex."

Freud's picture of the child is remarkably similar to that which St. Augustine has given. One of the main proofs that Augustine gives for the inherent sinfulness

of man is to point out the viciousness of the little child.
His reasoning is that man must be inherently evil since
the child is evil before it has a chance to learn evilness
from others and to be corrupted by bad examples. Freud,
like Augustine, does not emphasize those qualities in
the child which would at least balance this picture:
the child's spontaneity, its ability to respond, its delicate
judgment of people, its ability to recognize the attitudes
of others regardless of what they say, its unceasing effort to grasp the world; in short, all those qualities which
make us admire and love children and which have given
rise to the idea that the childlike qualities in the adult
belong among his most precious possessions. There are
numerous reasons why Freud puts all the emphasis on
the evil aspects of the child. One reason is that the Victorian age had created the illusion or the fiction of the
"innocent" child. It was supposed to have no sexual
strivings nor any other "bad" impulses. When Freud
attacked this convenient fiction, he was accused of be-
smirching the innocence of the child and of attacking
one of the supreme values the Victorian family believed
in. That Freud in this battle went to the other extreme
of giving a one-sided picture of the evilness of the child
is understandable.

Another reason for Freud's evaluation of the child
lies in the fact that, to Freud, one function of society is
to make man repress his immoral and asocial strivings,
producing by this repression socially valuable traits; this
transformation of evil into good operates through mechanisms which Freud calls "reaction formation" and "sublimation." The repression of an evil impulse, like sadism,

for instance, leads to the formation of an opposite impulse, like benevolence, the function of which is, dynamically speaking, to keep the repressed sadism from being expressed in thought, action, or feeling. By sublimation Freud refers to the phenomenon that the evil impulse is separated from its original asocial aims and used for higher and culturally valuable purposes. An illustration is a man who has sublimated his impulse to hurt into the valuable art of surgery. Freud holds that the benevolent, loving, constructive impulses in man are not primary; he claims that they are a secondary production arising from the necessity to repress his originally evil strivings. Culture is understood as being the result of such repression. In his original state Freud's "man," in contrast to Rousseau's, is possessed by evil impulses. The more society develops and forces him to repress these impulses, the more he learns to build reaction formations and sublimations. The higher the cultural development, the higher is the degree of repression. However, since man's capacity for reaction formations and sublimations is limited, this increasing repression often fails to be successful; the original strivings come to life and, since they cannot be acted upon overtly, lead to neurotic symptoms. Thus Freud assumes that man is confronted with an unavoidable alternative. The higher the cultural development the more repression and the more neurosis.

This concept makes it necessary to assume that the child remains essentially immoral as long as it is not controlled by social demands; that even this control never does away with the bulk of these evil impulses, which continue to live an underground existence.

Still another reason made Freud stress the irrationality of the child. As a result of analyzing his own dreams he was struck by the fact that even in a normal, mentally healthy adult such irrational strivings as hate, jealousy and ambition can be found. In the late 'nineties and the beginning of this century, a sharp demarcation line was felt to exist between the sick and the healthy. It was inconceivable that a normal, respectable citizen should or could harbor the many "crazy" impulses exhibited by his dreams. How could one explain the presence of these impulses in his dreams without destroying the concept of this healthy, "normal" adult? Freud found a solution to this difficulty in the assumption that these irrational strivings which appeared in dreams were expressions of the child in him, which was still alive and speaking up in dreams. Freud's theoretical construction was that certain of the child's impulses became repressed, lived an underground existence in the unconscious, and appeared in the dream, although distorted and veiled by the adult's need not to be fully aware of them even when he was asleep. I quote one of Freud's dreams, which he analyzed in his book on dream interpretation as an illustration for this point:

I. My friend R. is my uncle—I have a great affection for him.

II. I see before me his face, somewhat altered. It seems to be elongated; a yellow beard, which surrounds it, is seen with peculiar distinctness.

Then follow the other two portions of the dream, again a thought and an image, which I omit.

The interpretation of this dream was arrived at in the following manner:

> When I recollected the dream in the course of the morning, I laughed outright and said, "The dream is nonsense." But I could not get it out of my mind, and I was pursued by it all day, until at last, in the evening, I reproached myself in these words: "If in the course of a dream interpretation one of your patients could find nothing better to say than 'That is nonsense,' you would reprove him, and you would suspect that behind the dream there was hidden some disagreeable affair, the exposure of which he wanted to spare himself. Apply the same thing to your own case; your opinion that the dream is nonsense probably signifies merely an inner resistance to its interpretation. Don't let yourself be put off." I then proceeded with the interpretation.

> "R. is my uncle." What can that mean? I had only one uncle, my uncle Joseph.[1] His story, to be sure, was a sad one.

> Once more than thirty years ago, hoping to make money, he allowed himself to be involved in transactions of a kind which the law

[1] It is astonishing to see how my memory here restricts itself —in the waking state!—for the purposes of analysis. I have known five of my uncles, and I loved and honoured one of them. But at the moment when I overcame my resistance to the interpretation of the dream, I said to myself: "I have only one uncle, the one who is intended in the dream."

punishes severely, and paid the penalty. My father, whose hair turned grey with grief within a few days, used always to say that uncle Joseph had never been a bad man, but, after all, he was a simpleton. If, then, my friend R. is my uncle Joseph, that is equivalent to saying: "R. is a simpleton." Hardly credible, and very disagreeable! But there is the face that I saw in the dream, with its elongated features and its yellow beard. My uncle actually had such a face—long and framed in a handsome yellow beard. My friend R. was extremely swarthy, but when black-haired people begin to grow grey they pay for the glory of their youth. Their black beards undergo an unpleasant change of colour, hair by hair; first they turn a reddish brown, then a yellowish brown, and then definitely grey. My friend R.'s beard is now in this stage; so, for that matter, is my own, a fact which I note with regret. The face that I see in my dream is at once that of my friend R. and that of my uncle. It is like one of those composite photographs of Galton's; in order to emphasize family resemblances Galton had several faces photographed on the same plate. No doubt is now possible; it is really my opinion that my friend R. is a simpleton—like my uncle Joseph.

I still have no idea for what purpose I have worked out this relationship. It is certainly one to which I must unreservedly object. Yet it is not very profound, for my uncle was a criminal, and my friend R. is not, except in so far as he was once fined for knocking down an apprentice with his bicycle. Can I be thinking of this offence? That would make the comparison ridiculous. Here I recollect another conversation, which I had some days ago with another colleague, N.; as a matter of fact, on the same subject. I met N. in the street; he, too, has been nominated for a professorship, and having heard that I had been similarly honoured he congratulated me. I refused his congratulations, saying: "You are the last man to jest about the matter, for you know from your own experience what the nomination is worth." Thereupon he said, though probably not in earnest: "You can't be sure of that. There is a special objection in my case. Don't you know that a woman once brought a criminal accusation against me? I need hardly assure you that the matter was put right. It was a mean attempt at blackmail, and it was all I could do to save the plaintiff from punishment. But it may be that the affair is remembered against me at the Ministry. You, on the other hand, are above reproach." Here, then, I have the criminal, and at the same time interpretation and tendency of my dream. My uncle Joseph represents both of my colleagues who have not been appointed to the professorship—the one as a simpleton, the other as a criminal. Now, too, I know for what purpose I need this representation. If denominational considerations are a determining factor in the postponement of my two friends' appointment, then my own appointment is likewise in jeopardy. But if I can refer the rejection of my two friends to other causes, which do not apply to my own case, my hopes are unaffected. This is the procedure followed by my dream: it makes the one friend, R., a simpleton, and the other, N., a criminal. But since I am neither one nor the other, there is nothing in common between us. I have a right to enjoy my appointment to the title of professor, and have avoided the distressing application to my own case of the information which the official gave to my friend R.

I must pursue the interpretation of this dream still further; for I have a feeling that it is not yet satisfactorily elucidated. I still feel disquieted by the ease with which I have degraded two respected colleagues in order to clear my own way to the professorship. My dissatisfaction with this procedure has, of course, been mitigated since I have learned to estimate the testimony of dreams at its true value. I should contradict anyone who suggested that I really considered R. a simpleton, or that I did not believe N.'s account of the blackmailing incident. Nevertheless, I repeat, it still seems to me that the dream requires further elucidation.

I remember now that the dream contained yet another portion which has hitherto been ignored by the interpretation. After it occurred to me that my friend R. was my uncle, I felt in the dream a great affection for him. To whom is this feeling directed? For my uncle Joseph, of course, I have never had any feelings of affection. R. has for many years been a dearly loved friend, but if I were to go to him and express my affection for him in terms approaching the degree of affection which I felt in the dream he would undoubtedly be surprised. My affection, if it was for him, seems false and exaggerated, as does my judgment of his intellectual qualities, which I expressed by merging his personality in that of my uncle; but exaggerated in the opposite direction. Now, however, a new state of affairs dawns upon me. The affection in the dream does not belong to the latent content, to the thoughts behind the dream; it stands in opposition to this content; it is calculated to conceal the knowledge conveyed by the interpretation. Probably this is precisely its function. I remember with what reluctance I undertook the interpretation, how long I tried to postpone it, and how I declared the dream to be sheer nonsense. I know from my psychoanalytic practice how such a condemnation is to be interpreted. It has no informative value, but merely expresses an affect. If my little daughter does not like an apple which is offered her, she asserts that the apple is bitter, without even tasting it. If my patients behave thus, I know that we are dealing with an idea which they are trying to repress. The same thing applies to my dream. I do not want to interpret

it because there is something in the interpretation to which I object. After the interpretation of the dream is completed, I discover
what it was to which I objected; it was the
assertion that R. is a simpleton. I can refer the
affection which I feel for R. not to the latent
dream-thoughts, but rather to this unwilling-
ness of mine. If my dream, as compared with
its latent content, is disguised at this point
and actually misrepresents things by producing the opposites, then the manifest affection
in the dream serves the purpose of the mis-
representation; in other words, the distortion
is here shown to be intentional—it is a means
of *disguise*. My dream-thoughts of R. are de-
rogatory, and so that I may not become aware
of this the very opposite of defamation—a tender affection for him—enters into the dream.[2]

I shall now continue the interpretation of
a dream which has already proved instructive:
I refer to the dream in which my friend R. is
my uncle. We have carried its interpretation
far enough for the wish-motive—the wish to
be appointed professor—to assert itself palpa-
bly; and we have explained the affection felt
for my friend R. in the dream as the outcome
of opposition to, and defiance of, the two colleagues who appear in the dream-thoughts.
The dream was my own; I may, therefore,
continue the analysis by stating that I did not

[2] *The Interpretation of Dreams* (London: George Allen & Unwin,
Ltd.), also found in *The Basic Writings of Sigmund Freud*, translated
and edited with an introduction by Dr. A. A. Brill (New York: The
Modern Library, 1938), pp. 220–223.

feel quite satisfied with the solution arrived at. I knew that my opinion of these colleagues, who were so badly treated in my dream-thoughts, would have been expressed in very different language in my waking life; the intensity of the wish that I might not share their fate as regards the appointment seemed to me too slight fully to account for the discrepancy between my dream opinion and my waking opinion. If the desire to be addressed by another title were really so intense, it would be proof of a morbid ambition, which I do not think I cherish, and which I believe I was far from entertaining. I do not know how others who think they know me would judge me; perhaps I really was ambitious; but if I was, my ambition has long since been transferred to objects other than the rank and title of Professor extraordinarius.

Whence, then, the ambition which the dream has ascribed to me? Here I am reminded of a story which I heard often in my childhood, that at my birth an old peasant woman had prophesied to my happy mother (whose first-born I was) that she had brought a great man into the world. Such prophecies must be made very frequently; there are so many happy and expectant mothers, and so many old peasant women, and other old women who, since their mundane powers have deserted them, turn their eyes toward the future; and the prophetess is not likely to suffer for her prophecies. Is it possible that my thirst

for greatness has originated from this source?
But here I recollect an impression from the
later years of my childhood, which might
serve even better as an explanation. One evening, at a restaurant on the Prater, where my
parents were accustomed to take me when I
was eleven or twelve years of age, we noticed
a man who was going from table to table and,
for a small sum, improvising verses upon any
subject that was given him. I was sent to bring
the poet to our table, and he showed his grat-
itude. Before asking for a subject he threw off
a few rhymes about myself, and told us that,
if he could trust his inspiration, I should probably one day become a "minister." I can still
distinctly remember the impression produced
by this second prophecy. It was in the days of
the "bourgeois Ministry"; my father had recently brought home the portraits of the bourgeois university graduates, Herbst, Giskra,
Unger, Berger and others, and we illuminated
the house in their honour. There were even
Jews among them; so that every diligent Jewish schoolboy carried a ministerial portfolio
in his satchel. The impression of that time
must be responsible for the fact that until
shortly before I went to the university I
wanted to study jurisprudence, and changed
my mind only at the last moment. A medical
man has no chance of becoming a minister.
And now for my dream: It is only now that I
begin to see that it translates me from the
sombre present to the hopeful days of the

bourgeois Ministry, and completely fulfills what was then my youthful ambition. In treating my two estimable and learned colleagues, merely because they are Jews, so badly, one as though he were a simpleton, and the other as though he were a criminal, I am acting as though I were the Minister; I have put myself in his place. What a revenge I take upon his Excellency! He refuses to appoint me Professor extraordinarius, and so in my dream I put myself in his place.[3]

The interpretation of this dream is an excellent illustration for Freud's tendency to consider irrational strivings like ambition as incompatible with the grown-up personality and therefore as being part of the child in him. The dream shows clearly the ambition Freud had at the time of this dream. But Freud flatly denies that he could harbor such marked ambition. In fact he gives a good illustration of the process of rationalization, which he has described so brilliantly. His reasoning is: "If the desire to be addressed by another title [by this expression he tends to minimize the real point, namely, the prestige which the title carries with it] were really so intense, it would be a proof of a morbid ambition." And of this ambition he says that he does not think he cherishes it. But even if others would judge him to have such an ambition, he asserts that it could not possibly be for the title of full professor. He therefore is forced to assume that this ambition belonged to his childhood desires and not to his present personality.

[3] *Ibid.*, pp. 256, 257, 258.

While it is, of course, true that strivings like ambition develop in the character of the child and have their roots in the early part of life, it is not true that they are something separate from the present personality. Speaking of a normal person like himself, Freud feels compelled to draw the sharp distinction between the child in him and himself. It is largely due to his influence that this sharp demarcation line is not felt to exist today. There is wide recognition of the fact that even the normal person can be motivated by all sorts of irrational desires and that they are *his* wishes even though they stem from his early development.

So far we have shown one aspect of Freud's theory of dreams. Dreams are understood to be the hallucinatory fulfillment of irrational wishes and particularly sexual wishes which have originated in our early childhood and have not been fully transformed into reaction formations or sublimations. These wishes are expressed as being fulfilled when our conscious control is weakened, as is the case in sleep. However, if we would permit ourselves to live out the fulfillment of these irrational desires in our dreams, dreams would not be so puzzling and confusing. We rarely dream that we commit murder or incest or any other kind of crime, and even if we do so, we do nōt enjoy the fulfillment of these wishes in our dreams. In order to explain this phenomenon Freud assumes that in our sleep life the moral censor in ourselves is half asleep, too. Thus thoughts and fantasies are permitted to enter into our sleep consciousness which otherwise are completely shut out. But the censor is only half asleep. He is sufficiently awake to make it impossible for the forbidden thoughts to appear clearly and unmistakably. If the function of the dream is to preserve our sleep, the irrational wishes that appear in the dream must be sufficiently disguised to deceive the censor. Like the neurotic symptoms, they are a compromise between the repressed forces of the id and the repressing force of the censoring superego. It happens sometimes that this mechanism of distortion does not work properly, and our dream becomes too clear to be overlooked by the censor—and we wake up. Consequently, Freud's assumption is that the main characteristic of dream language is the process of disguise and distortion of the irrational wishes which permits us to go on sleeping undisturbed. This idea has an important bearing on Freud's concept of symbolism. He believes that the main function of the symbol is to disguise and distort the underlying wish. *Symbolic language is conceived as a "secret code"; dream interpretation as the work of deciphering it.*

The assumption both of the irrational infantile nature of the dream content and of the distorting function of dream-work has led to a much narrower concept of dream language than the one I have suggested in the discussion of symbolic language. Symbolic language, to Freud, is not a language which can express any kind of feeling and thought in a particular way, but one which expresses only certain primitive instinctual desires. The vast majority of symbols are of a sexual nature. The male genital is symbolized by sticks, trees, umbrellas, knives, pencils, hammers, airplanes, and many other objects which can represent it either by their shape or by their function. The female genital is represented in the same manner by caves, bottles, boxes, doors, jewel cases, gardens, flowers, etc. Sexual pleasure is represented by activities like dancing, riding, climbing, flying. The falling out of hair or teeth is a symbolic representation of castration. Aside from sexual elements, symbols are expressive of the fundamental experiences of the little child. Father and mother are symbolized as king and queen or emperor and empress, children as little animals, death as a journey.

In his dream interpretation, however, Freud makes more use of the accidental symbols than of the universal symbols. He holds that in order to interpret the dream we have to cut it up into its several pieces and thus do away with its semi-logical sequence. We then try to associate to each element of the dream and to substitute the thoughts that come into our mind in this process of association for the parts that appeared in the dream. If we put together the thoughts arrived at by free association, we arrive at a new text which has an inner consistency and logic and divulges to us the true meaning of the dream.

This true dream, which is the expression of our hidden desires, Freud calls the "latent dream." The distorted version of the dream as we remember it is the "manifest dream" and the process of distortion and disguise is the "dream-work." The main mechanisms through which the dream-work translates the latent into the manisfest dream are condensation, displacement and secondary elaboration. By condensation Freud refers to the fact that the manifest dream is much shorter than the latent dream. It leaves out a number of elements of the latent dream, combines fragments of various elements, and condenses them into one new element in the manifest dream. If one dreams, for instance, of an authoritative male figure one is afraid of, one might in the manifest dream see a man whose hair looks like that of one's father, whose face is like the face of a frightening schoolteacher, and who is dressed like one's boss. Or if one dreams of a situation in which one felt sad and unhappy, one might dream of a house which by its roof represents a house in which one had the same experience of sadness and by the shape of the room another house connected with the same emotional experience. In the manifest dream both elements appear in the composite picture of one house. These examples show that only those elements are condensed into one picture which in the emotional content are identical. In view of the nature of symbolic language, the process of condensation can be readily understood. While with reference to external reality the fact that two people or two things are different is important, from the standpoint of internal reality this fact is of no consequence. What matters is that they are related to and expressive of the same inner experience.

By displacement Freud refers to the fact that an element of the latent dream, and often a very important one, is expressed by a remote element in the manifest dream and usually one which appears to be quite unimportant. As a result, the manifest dream often treats the really important elements as if they were of no particular significance and thus disguises the true meaning of the dream.

✓ By secondary elaboration Freud understands that part of the dream-work which completes the process of disguise. Gaps in the manifest dream are filled in, inconsistencies are repaired, with the result that the manifest dream assumes the form of a logical consistent story behind the façade of which the exciting and dramatic dream play is hidden.

Freud mentions two other factors which make the understanding of the dream difficult and add to the distorting function of the dream-work. One is that elements often stand for the very opposite. To be clothed may symbolize nakedness, to be rich may stand for being poor, and the feeling of particular affection may stand for the feeling of hostility and rage. The other factor is that the manifest dream does not express logical relations between its various elements. It has no "but," "therefore," "because," "if," but expresses these logical relations in the relation between the pictorial images. The dreamer may, for instance, dream of a person standing up and raising his arm and then being transformed into a chicken. In waking language the dream thought would be expressed as meaning, "He gives the appearance of being strong, *but* he is really weak and cowardly like a chicken." In the manifest dream this logical relation is expressed by a sequence of the two images.

One important addition must be made to this brief description of Freud's dream theory. The emphasis on the infantile nature of the dream content could lead one to believe that Freud does not assume any important link between the dream and the present but only one with the past. This is not at all the case, however. It is Freud's assumption that the dream is always stimulated by a present event, usually on the day or the evening before the dream occurs. But a dream is provoked only by such events which are related to early infantile strivings. The energy for the creation of the dream stems from the intensity of the infantile experience, but the dream would not come into existence were it not for the recent event that touched upon the earlier experience and made it possible for it to come to life at that particular moment. A simple illustration will clarify this point: A man who works under an authoritarian boss may be unduly afraid of this man because of the fear he had of his father as a child. The night after the day on which his boss criticized him for one reason or another he has a nightmare in which he sees a figure which is a mixed compositum of his father and his boss trying to kill him. Had he not been afraid of his father as a child, his boss's annoyance would not have frightened him. But if his boss had not been annoyed that day, this deep-seated fear would not have been mobilized and the dream would not have occurred.

The reader will get a better idea of Freud's method of dream interpretation by seeing how the principles we have just presented are applied by Freud in his interpretation of specific dreams. The first of the two following dreams is centered around a universal symbol: nakedness. The second dream uses almost exclusively accidental symbols.

The Embarrassment-Dream of Nakedness

In a dream in which one is naked or scantily clad in the presence of strangers, it sometimes happens that one is not in the least ashamed of one's condition. But the dream of nakedness demands our attention only when shame and embarrassment are felt in it, when one wishes to escape or to hide, and when one feels the strange inhibition of being unable to stir from the spot, and of being utterly powerless to alter the painful situation. It is only in this connection that the dream is typical; otherwise the nucleus of its content may be involved in all sorts of other connections, or may be replaced by individual amplifications. The essential point is that one has a painful feeling of shame, and is anxious to hide one's nakedness, usually by means of locomotion, but is absolutely unable to do so. I believe that the great majority of my readers will at some time have found themselves in this situation in a dream.

The nature and manner of the exposure is usually rather vague. The dreamer will say, perhaps, "I was in my chemise," but this is rarely a clear image; in most cases the lack of clothing is so indeterminate that it is described in narrating the dream by an alternative: "I was in my chemise or my petticoat." As a rule the deficiency in clothing is not serious enough to justify the feeling of shame attached to it. For a man who has served in the army, nakedness is often replaced by a manner of dressing that is contrary to regulations. "I was in the street without my sabre, and I saw some officers approaching," or "I had no collar," or "I was wearing checked civilian trousers," etc.

The persons before whom one is ashamed are almost always strangers, whose faces remain indeterminate. It never happens in the typical dream that one is reproved or even noticed on account of the lack of clothing which causes one such embarrassment. On the contrary, the people in the dream appear to be quite indifferent; or, as I was able to note in one particularly vivid dream, they have stiff and solemn expressions. This gives us food for thought.

The dreamer's embarrassment and the spectator's indifference constitute a contradiction such as often occurs in dreams. It would be more in keeping with the dreamer's feelings if the strangers were to look at him in astonishment, or were to laugh at him, or be outraged. I think, however, that this obnoxious feature has been displaced by wish-fulfilment while the embarrassment is for some reason retained, so that the two components are not in agreement. We have an interesting proof that the dream which is partially distorted by wish-fulfilment has not been properly understood; for it has been made the basis of a fairy tale familiar to us all in Andersen's version of "The Emperor's New Clothes," and it has more recently received

poetical treatment by Fulda in "The Talis-
man." In Andersen's fairy tale we are told of
two impostors who weave a costly garment for
the Emperor, which shall, however, be visible
only to the good and true. The Emperor goes
forth clad in this invisible garment, and since
the imaginary fabric serves as a sort of touch-
stone, the people are frightened into behaving
as though they did not notice the Emperor's
nakedness.

But this is really the situation in our
dream. It is not very venturesome to assume
that the unintelligible dream content has provided an incentive to invent a state of undress
which gives meaning to the situation present
in the memory. This situation is thereby
robbed of its original meaning and made to
serve alien ends. But we shall see that such a
misunderstanding of the dream-content often
occurs through the conscious activity of a second psychic system, and is to be recognized as
a factor of the final form of the dream; and
further, that in the development of obses-
sions and phobias similar misunderstandings
—still, of course, within the same psychic personality—play a decisive part. It is even possible to specify whence the material for the
fresh interpretation of the dream is taken.
The impostor is the dream, the Emperor is
the dreamer himself, and the moralizing tendency betrays a hazy knowledge of the fact that
there is a question, in the latent dream-content, of forbidden wishes, victims of repres-

sion. The connection in which dreams appear during my analyses of neurotics proves beyond a doubt that a memory of the dreamer's earliest childhood lies at the foundation of the dream. Only in our childhood was there a time when we were seen by our relatives, as well as by strange nurses, servants and visitors, in a state of insufficient clothing, and at the same time we were not ashamed of our nakedness.* In the case of many rather older children it may be observed that being undressed has an exciting effect upon them, instead of making them feel ashamed. they laugh, leap about, slap or thump their own bodies; the mother, or whoever is present, scolds them, saying, "Fie, that is shameful—you mustn't do that!" Children often show a desire to display themselves; it is hardly possible to pass through a village in country districts without meeting a two- or three-year-old child who lifts up his or her blouse or frock before the traveller, possibly in his honour. One of my patients has retained in his conscious memory a scene from his eighth year, in which, after undressing for bed, he wanted to dance into his little sister's room in his shirt, but was prevented by the servant. In the history of the childhood of neurotics exposure before children of the opposite sex plays a prominent part; in paranoia the delusion of

* The child appears in the fairy tale also, for there a little child suddenly cries out, "But he hasn't anything on at all!"

being observed while dressing or undressing may be directly traced to these experiences; and among those who have remained perverse there is a class in whom the childish impulse is accentuated into a symptom: the class of *exhibitionists*.

This age of childhood, in which the sense of shame is unknown, seems a paradise when we look back upon it later, and paradise itself is nothing but the mass-phantasy of the childhood of the individual. This is why in paradise men are naked and unashamed, until the moment arrives when shame and fear awaken; expulsion follows, and sexual life and cultural development begin. Into this paradise dreams can take us back every night; we have already ventured the conjecture that the impressions of our earliest childhood (from the prehistoric period until about the end of the third year) crave reproduction for their own sake, perhaps without further reference to their content, so that their repetition, is a wish-fulfilment. Dreams of nakedness, then, are exhibition-dreams.

The nucleus of an exhibition-dream is furnished by one's own person, which is seen not as that of a child, but as it exists in the present, and by the idea of scanty clothing which emerges indistinctly, owing to the superimposition of so many later situations of being partially clothed, or out of consideration for the censorship; to these elements are added the persons in whose presence one is ashamed. I know of no example in which the actual spectators of these infantile exhibitions reappear in a dream; for a dream is hardly ever a simple recollection. Strangely enough, those persons who are the objects of our sexual interest in childhood are omitted from all reproductions, in dreams, in hysteria or in obsessional neurosis; paranoia alone restores the spectators, and is fanatically convinced of their presence, although they remain unseen. The substitute for these persons offered by the dream, the "number of strangers" who take no notice of the spectacle offered them, is precisely the *counter-wish* to that single intimately known person for whom the exposure was intended. "A number of strangers," moreover, often occur in dreams in all sorts of other connections; as a *counter-wish* they always signify "a secret." It will be seen that even that restitution of the old state of affairs that occurs in paranoia complies with this counter-tendency. One is no longer alone; one is quite positively being watched; but the spectators are "a number of strange, curiously indeterminate people."

Furthermore, repression finds a place in the exhibition-dream. For the disagreeable sensation of the dream is, of course, the reaction on the part of the second psychic instance to the fact that the exhibitionistic scene which has been condemned by the censorship has nevertheless succeeded in presenting itself.

The only way to avoid this sensation would be to refrain from reviving the scene.[4]

Dream of the Botanical Monograph

I have written a monograph on a certain plant. The book lies before me; I am just turning over a folded coloured plate. A dried specimen of the plant, as though from a herbarium, is bound up with every copy.

Analysis:

In the morning I saw in a bookseller's window a volume entitled *The Genus Cyclamen*, apparently a monograph on this plant.

The cyclamen is my wife's favourite flower. I reproach myself for remembering so seldom to bring her flowers, as she would like me to do. In connection with the theme of giving her flowers, I am reminded of a story which I recently told some friends of mine in proof of my assertion that we often forget in obedience to a purpose of the unconscious, and that forgetfulness always enables us to form a deduction about the secret disposition of the forgetful person. A young woman who has been accustomed to receive a bouquet of flowers from her husband on her birthday misses this token of affection on one of her birthdays, and bursts into tears. The husband comes in, and cannot understand why she is crying until she tells him: "Today is my birthday." He claps his hand to his forehead and exclaims: "Oh, forgive me, I had completely forgotten it!"

[4] *Ibid.*, pp. 292–295.

and proposes to go out immediately in order to get her flowers. But she refuses to be consoled, for she sees in her husband's forgetfulness a proof that she no longer plays the same part in his thoughts as she formerly did. This Frau L. met my wife two days ago, told her that she was feeling well, and asked after me. Some years ago she was a patient of mine.

Supplementary facts: I did once actually write something like a monograph on a plant, namely, an essay on the coca plant, which attracted the attention of K. Koller to the anaesthetic properties of cocaine. I had hinted that the alkaloid might be employed as an anaesthetic, but I was not thorough enough to pursue the matter further. It occurs to me, too, that on the morning of the day following the dream (for the interpretation of which I did not find time until the evening) I had thought of cocaine in a kind of day-dream. If I were ever afflicted with glaucoma, I would go to Berlin, and there undergo an operation, incognito, in the house of my Berlin friend, at the hands of a surgeon whom he would recommend. The surgeon, who would not know the name of his patient, would boast as usual, how easy these operations had become since the introduction of cocaine; and I should not betray the fact that I myself had a share in this discovery. With this phantasy were connected thoughts of how awkward it really is for a physician to claim the professional services of a colleague. I should be able to pay the Berlin

eye specialist, who did not know me, like anyone else. Only after recalling this day-dream
do I realize that there is concealed behind it
the memory of a definite event. Shortly after
Koller's discovery, my father contracted glaucoma; he was operated on by my friend Dr.
Koenigstein, the eye specialist. Dr. Koller was
in charge of the cocaine anaesthetization, and
he made the remark that on this occasion all
the three persons who had been responsible
for the introduction of cocaine had been
brought together.

My thoughts now pass on to the time
when I was last reminded of the history of cocaine. This was a few days earlier, when I received a *Festschrift*, a publication in which
grateful pupils had commemorated the jubi-
lee of their teacher and laboratory director.
Among the titles to fame of persons connected
with the laboratory I found a note to the effect that the discovery of the anaesthetic properties of cocaine had been due to K. Koller.
Now I suddenly become aware that the dream
is connected with an experience of the previous evening. I had just accompanied Dr.
Koenigstein to his home, and had entered into
a discussion of a subject which excites me
greatly whenever it is mentioned. While I was
talking with him in the entrance-hall Professor Gartner and his young wife came up. I
could not refrain from congratulating them
both upon their *blooming* appearance. Now
Professor Gartner is one of the authors of the

Festschrift of which I have just spoken, and he may well have reminded me of it. And Frau L., of whose birthday disappointment I spoke a little way back, had been mentioned, though of course in another connection, in my conversation with Dr. Koenigstein.

I shall now try to elucidate the other determinants of the dream-content. A *dried specimen* of the plant accompanies the monograph, as though it were a *herbarium*. And herbarium reminds me of the "gymnasium." The director of our "gymnasium" once called the pupils of the upper classes together, in order that they might examine and clean the "gymnasium" herbarium. Small insects had been found—*book-worms*. The director seemed to have little confidence in my ability to assist, for he entrusted me with only a few of the pages. I know to this day that there were crucifers on them. My interest in botany was never very great. At my preliminary examination in botany I was required to identify a crucifer, and failed to recognize it; had not my theoretical knowledge come to my aid, I should have fared badly indeed. Crucifers suggest composites. The artichoke is really a composite, and in actual fact one which I might call my *favourite flower*. My wife, more thoughtful than I, often brings this favourite flower of mine home from the market.

I see the monograph which I have written lying before me. Here again there is an association. My friend wrote to me yesterday from Berlin: "I am thinking a great deal about your dream-book. I see it lying before me, completed, and I turn the pages." How I envied him this power of vision! If only I could see it lying before me, already completed!

The folded coloured plate. When I was a medical student I suffered a sort of craze for studying monographs exclusively. In spite of my limited means, I subscribed to a number of the medical periodicals, whose *coloured plates* afforded me much delight. I was rather proud of this inclination to thoroughness. When I subsequently began to publish books myself, I had to draw the plates for my own treatises, and I remember one of them turned out so badly that a well-meaning colleague ridiculed me for it. With this is associated, I do not exactly know how, a very early memory of my childhood. My father, by way of a jest, once gave my elder sister and myself a book containing *coloured plates* (the book was a narrative of a journey through Persia) in order that we might destroy it. From an educational point of view this was hardly to be commended. I was at the time five years old, and my sister less than three, and the picture of us two children blissfully tearing the book to pieces (I should add, like an *artichoke,* leaf by leaf), is almost the only one from this period of my life which has remained vivid in my memory. When I afterwards became a student, I developed a conspicuous fondness for

collecting and possessing books (an analogy to
the inclination for studying from monographs,
a hobby alluded to in my dream thoughts, in
connection with cyclamen and artichoke). I
became a *book-worm* (cf. herbarium). Ever
since I have been engaged in introspection I
have always traced this earliest passion of my
life to this impression of my childhood: or
rather, I have recognized in this childish scene
a "screen or concealing memory" for my subsequent bibliophilia. And of course I learned
at an early age that our passions often become
our misfortunes. When I was seventeen, I ran
up a very considerable account at the bookseller's, with no means with which to settle it,
and my father would hardly accept it as an ex-
cuse that my passion was at least a respectable
one. But the mention of this experience of my
youth brings me back to my conversation with
my friend Dr. Koenigstein on the evening
preceding the dream; for one of the themes of
this conversation was the same old reproach—
that I am much too absorbed in my *hobbies*.

For reasons which are not relevant here I
shall not continue the interpretation of this
dream, but will merely indicate the path
which leads to it. In the course of the interpretation I was reminded of my conversation
with Dr. Koenigstein, and, indeed, of more
than one portion of it. When I consider the
subjects touched upon in this conversation,
the meaning of the dream immediately becomes clear to me. All the trains of thought

which have been started—my own inclinations, and those of my wife, the cocaine, the awkwardness of securing medical treatment from one's own colleagues, my preference for monographical studies, and my neglect of certain subjects, such as botany—all these are continued in and lead up to one branch or another of this widely ramified conversation. The dream once more assumes the character of a justification, of a plea for my rights (like the dream of Irma's injection, the first to be analyzed); it even continues the theme which that dream introduced, and discusses it in association with the new subject-matter which has been added in the interval between the two dreams. Even the dream's apparently indifferent form of expression at once acquires a meaning. Now it means: "I am indeed the man who has written that valuable and successful treatise (on cocaine)," just as previously I declared in self-justification: "I am after all a thorough and industrious student;" and in both instances I find the meaning: "I can allow myself this." But I may dispense with the further interpretation of the dream, because my only purpose in recording it was to examine the relation of the dream content to the experience of the previous day which aroused it. As long as I know only the manifest content of this dream, only one relation to any impression of the day is obvious; but after I have completed the interpretation, a second source of the dream becomes apparent in another experience of the same day. The first of these impressions to which the dream refers is an indifferent one, a subordinate circumstance. I see a book in a shop window whose title holds me for a moment, but whose contents would hardly interest me. The second experience was of great psychic value; I talked earnestly with my friend, the eye specialist, for about an hour; I made allusions in this conversation which must have ruffled the feelings of both of us, and which in me awakened memories in connection with which I had a great variety of inner stimuli. Further, this conversation was broken off unfinished, because some acquaintances joined us. What, now, is the relation of these two impressions of the day to one another, and to the dream which followed during the night?

In the manifest dream-content I find merely an illusion to the indifferent impression, and I am thus able to reaffirm that the dream prefers to take up into its content experiences of a non-essential character. In the dream-interpretation, on the contrary, everything converges upon the important and justifiably disturbing event. If I judge the sense of the dream in the only correct way, according to the latent content which is brought to light in the analysis, I find that I have unwittingly lighted upon a new and important discovery. I see that the puzzling theory that the dream deals only with the worthless odds and ends of the day's experiences has no justification; I am

also compelled to contradict the assertion that
the psychic life of the waking state is not continued in the dream, and that hence, the
dream wastes our psychic energy on trivial
material. The very opposite is true; what has
claimed our attention during the day domi-
nates our dream-thoughts also, and we take
pains to dream only in connection with such
matters as have given us food for thought during the day.

Perhaps the most immediate explanation
of the fact that I dream of the indifferent impression of the day, while the impression
which has with good reason excited me causes
me to dream, is that here again we are dealing
with the phenomenon of dream-distortion,
which we have referred to as a psychic force
playing the part of a censorship. The recollection of the monograph on the genus cyclamen
is utilized as though it were an *allusion* to the
conversation with my friend, just as the mention of my patient's friend in the dream of the
deferred supper is represented by the allusion
"smoked salmon." The only question is, by
what intermediate links can the impression
of the monograph come to assume the relation
of allusion to the conversation with the eye
specialist, since such a relation is not at first
perceptible? . . . In our . . . example we are
dealing with two entirely separate impressions,
which at first glance seem to have nothing in
common, except indeed that they occur on the
same day. The monograph attracts my atten-

tion in the morning: in the evening I take part in the conversation. The answer furnished by the analysis is as follows: Such relations between the two impressions as do not exist from the first are established subsequently between the idea-content of the one impression and the idea-content of the other. I have already picked out the intermediate links emphasized in the course of writing the analysis. Only under some outside influence, perhaps the recollection of the flowers missed by Frau L., would the idea of the monograph on the cyclamen have attached itself to the idea that the cyclamen is my wife's favourite flower. I do not believe that these inconspicuous thoughts would have sufficed to evoke a dream.

> "There needs no ghost, my lord, come
>   from the grave
> To tell us this,"

as we read in Hamlet. But behold! in the analysis I am reminded that the name of the man who interrupted our conversation was *Gartner* (gardner), and that I thought his wife looked *blooming;* indeed now I even remember that one of my female patients, who bears the pretty name of *Flora,* was for a time the main subject of our conversation. It must have happened that by means of these intermediate links from the sphere of botanical ideas the association was effected between the two events of the day, the indifferent one and the stimulating one. Other relations were then established, that of cocaine for example, which can with perfect appropriateness form a link between the person of Dr. Koenigstein and the botanical monograph which I have written, and thus secure the fusion of the two circles of ideas, so that now a portion of the first experience may be used as an allusion to the second.

I am prepared to find this explanation attacked as either arbitrary or artificial. What would have happened if Professor Gartner and his blooming wife had not appeared, and if the patient who was under discussion had been called, not Flora, but Anna? And yet the answer is not hard to find. If these thought-relations had not been available, others would probably have been selected. It is easy to establish relations of this sort, as the jocular questions and conundrums with which we amuse ourselves suffice to show. The range of wit is unlimited. To go a step farther: if no sufficiently fertile associations between the two impressions of the day could have been established, the dream would simply have followed a different course; another of the indifferent impressions of the day, such as come to us in multitudes and are forgotten, would have taken the place of the monograph in the dream, would have formed an association with the content of the conversation, and would have represented this in the dream. Since it was the impression of the monograph and no other that was fated to perform this function, this impression was probably that most suitable for the purpose. One need not, like Lessing's *Hanschen Schlau*, be astonished that "only the rich people of the world possess the most money." [5]

The two foregoing dreams give us an opportunity not only to study the application of Freud's general principles to specific dreams, but also to compare Freud's interpretation with the one I have suggested in the second chapter of this book. In the interpretation of the nakedness dream Freud follows the general principle as outlined above. The dream constitutes the fulfillment of infantile irrational wishes, but under the censor influence it distorts and disguises the wish-fulfillment. The irrational wish that is fulfilled is the exhibitionistic childhood wish to exhibit one's genitals. But our grown-up personality is afraid of such wishes and expresses embarrassment at the fulfillment of the wish that the infant in us harbors.

This interpretation is undoubtedly correct in many instances. But it is not always correct, because the contents of a dream are not necessarily of an infantile nature. Freud ignores the fact that nakedness can be a symbol of things other than sexual exhibitionism. Nakedness can, for instance, be a symbol of truthfulness. To be naked can stand for being oneself without pretense, and being clothed can stand for the expressions of thoughts and feelings which others expect us to have while they actually are not ours. The naked body can thus symbolize the real self; the clothes can symbolize the social self that feels and thinks in terms

[5] *Ibid.*, pp. 241–246.

of the current cultural pattern. If someone dreams of being naked, the dream may express his wish to be himself, to give up pretense, and his embarrassment in the dream may reflect the fear he has of the disapproval of others if he dares to be himself.

The interpretation of Andersen's fairy tale in connection with his interpretation of the nakedness dream is a good illustration of a misunderstanding of a fairy tale necessitated by Freud's assumption that fairy tales, like dreams and myths, are necessarily the expressions of repressed sexual desires. The fairy tale of the Emperor's new clothes is not the distorted expression of an exhibitionistic wish. It deals with an entirely different experience—our readiness to believe in the imaginary wonderful qualities of authorities and our inability to recognize their true stature. The child who is not yet sufficiently imbued with the awe of authority is the only one who can see that the Emperor is naked and does not wear invisible garments. Everybody else, impressed by the implicit threat that he is not good and true unless he sees the garment, yields to the suggestion and believes that he sees something which his eyes cannot possibly see. The story deals with the theme of debunking irrational claims of authorities and not with that of exhibitionism.

The dream about the botanical monograph is an excellent illustration for the many threads of associations that are woven into this very brief dream. Anyone who attempts to interpret dreams by following up the associations that come up with each single element of the dream cannot fail to be greatly impressed by the richness of associations, and by the almost miraculous way in which they are condensed into the dream text.

The disadvantage of the illustration is that Freud refrains from giving a full interpretation and mentions only one wish expressed in the dream, namely, that of justifying himself by pointing to his achievements. Again, if we do not insist that every dream is an expression of a wish-fulfillment but recognize that it may be expressive of any kind of mental activity, we would arrive at a different interpretation.

The central symbol of the dream is the dried flower. A dried and carefully preserved flower contains an element of contradiction. It is a flower, something standing for aliveness and beauty, but in being dried it has lost this very quality and has become an object of detached scientific study. Freud's associations to the dream point to this contradiction in the symbol. Freud mentions that the flower, cyclamen, the monograph about which he had seen in the bookseller's window, is his wife's favorite flower, and he reproaches himself for remembering so seldom to bring her flowers. In other words, the monograph about the cyclamen stirs up his feeling that he fails in that aspect of life which is symbolized by love and tenderness. All the other associations point in one direction, that of his ambition. The monograph reminds him of his work on cocaine and of his resentment at not being given sufficient credit for its discovery. He is reminded of the disappointment to his ego when the director of the school had little confidence in his ability to assist in cleaning the herbarium. And the colored plates remind him of another blow to his ego, the ridicule of his colleagues that one of the colored plates had turned out so badly.

The dream, then, seems to express a conflict which Freud feels sharply in the dream while he seems not to be aware of it in his waking life. He reproaches himself for having neglected that side of life which is expressed by the flower and by his wife for the sake of his ambition and his one-sided intellectual scientific orientation to the world. In fact, the dream is expressive of a deep contradiction in Freud's total personality and his lifework. The main subject matter of his interest and his studies is love and sex. But he is a puritan; if anything, we notice in him a Victorian aversion against sex and pleasure combined with a sad tolerance for man's weakness in this respect. He has dried the flower, made sex and love the object of scientific inspection and speculation, rather than leave it alive. The dream is expressive of the great paradox in Freud: he is not at all—as he has often been misinterpreted—the representative of the "sensuous-frivolous, immoral Viennese atmosphere" but, on the contrary, a puritan who could write so freely about sex and love because he had put them in a herbarium. His own interpretation tends to hide this very conflict by misreading the meaning of the dream.

Freud's interpretation of myths and fairy tales follows the same principle as his interpretation of dreams. The symbolism as we find it in myth is regarded by Freud as a regression to earlier stages of human development where certain activities like plowing and the creation of fire were invested with sexual libido. In the myth this early and now repressed libidinous satisfaction is expressed in "substitutive gratifications," which make it possible for man to restrict the satisfaction of instinctive desires to the realm of fantasy.

In the myth, as in the dream, the primitive impulses are not expressed overtly but in disguise. They deal with those strivings which Freud believed he had discovered as occurring regularly in the child's life, particularly incestuous wishes, sexual curiosity, and fear of castration. An illustration of this method of myth interpretation is Freud's interpretation of the Sphinx riddle. The Sphinx had stipulated that the plague that was threatening Thebes with extinction would cease only if someone could find the right answer to a riddle she was presenting. The riddle was: "What is it? It is first on four, then on two, then on three?" Freud considers the riddle and the answer, man, to be the disguise of another question that is foremost in the child's fantasy, the riddle: "Where do children come from?" The Sphinx's question is rooted in the sexual curiosity of the child, a curiosity discouraged and driven underground by parental authority. Thus, he has assumed, the Sphinx riddle is expressive of the deep-seated sexual curiosity inherent in man, but disguised as if it were an innocent intellectual pursuit far removed from the forbidden zone of sex.

Jung and Silberer, two of the most gifted of Freud's students, recognized early the one weakness in Freud's dream interpretation and tried to correct it. Silberer differentiated between what he called the "anagogic" and the "analytic" interpretation of the dream. Jung made the same point by differentiating between the "prospective" and the "retrospective" interpretation. They claimed that every dream represents wishes of the past, but that it is also oriented to the future and has the function of indicating the goals and aims of the dreamer. As Jung put it:

> Psyche is transition, hence necessarily to be defined under two aspects. On the one hand, the psyche gives a picture of the remnants and traces of the entire past, and, on the other, but expressed in the same picture, the outlines of the future, inasmuch as the psyche creates its own future.[6]

Jung and Silberer assumed that each dream had to be understood in both its anagogic and its analytic meaning, and there was some reason to expect that Freud might accept this modification. But if a compromise with Freud was aimed at, the attempt failed. Freud rigidly refused to accept any such modification and insisted that the only possible interpretation of a dream was that of the wish-fulfillment theory. After the split between the Jungian and the Freudian school had occurred, Jung tended to remove Freud's concepts from his system and replace them with new ones; then Jung's theory of dreams changed. While Freud was prone to rely mostly on free association and to understand the dream as an expression of infantile irrational desires, Jung dispensed more and more with free association and equally dogmatically tended to interpret the

[6] C. G. Jung, "On Psychological Understanding," *Journal of Abnormal Psychology*, 1915, p. 391.

dream as the expression of the wisdom of the unconscious.

This view fits into Jung's whole concept of the unconscious. He believes "that the unconscious mind is capable at times of assuming an intelligence and purposiveness which are superior to actual conscious insight." [7] Thus far I have no quarrel with this statement and it corresponds to my own experience with dream interpretation outlined above. But Jung proceeds from here to state that this fact is a "basic religious phenomenon and that the voice which speaks in our dreams is not our own but comes from a source transcending us." To the objection "that the thoughts which the voice represents are no more than the thoughts of the individual himself" he answers:

> That may be; but I would call a thought my own when *I* have thought it as I would call money my own when I have earned or acquired it in a conscious and legitimate way. If somebody gives me the money as a present, then I will certainly not say to my benefactor, "Thank you for my own money," although to a third person and afterwards I might say, "This is my own money." With the voice I am in a similar situation. The voice gives me certain contents, exactly as a friend would inform me of his ideas. It would be neither decent nor true to suggest that what he says are my own ideas.[8]

[7] C. G. Jung, *Psychology and Religion*, (New Haven: Yale University Press, 1938), p. 45.
[8] Ibid., p. 46.

He states the same point somewhere else even more clearly: "Man is never helped by what he thinks for himself but by revelations of wisdom greater than his own."

The difference between Jung's interpretation and my own can be summed up in this statement. There is agreement that we often are wiser and more decent in our sleep than in our waking life. Jung explains this phenomenon with the assumption of a source of revelation transcending us, while I believe that what we think in our sleep is *our* thinking, and that are good reasons for the fact that the influences we are submitted to in our waking life have in many respects a stultifying effect on our intellectual and moral accomplishments.

Again, the understanding of Jung's method will be facilitated by presenting a dream analysis of his own. The dream is taken from a series of over four hundred dreams which a patient of Jung's had written down. The dreamer is a Catholic by education but no longer a practicing one, nor is he interested in religious problems. This is one of his dreams:

> There are many houses which have a theatrical character, a sort of stage scenery. Somebody mentions the name of Bernard Shaw. It is also mentioned that the play which is to follow refers to a remote future. One of the houses is distinguished by a signboard with the following inscription:

> This is the universal Catholic church.
> It is the church of the Lord.

All those who feel themselves to be
instruments of the Lord may enter.

And below in smaller letters:

The church is founded by Jesus and Paul

—it is as if a firm boasted of its old standing. I
say to my friend, "Let us go in and have a
look." He replies, "I do not see why many
people should be together in order to have religious feelings." But I say, "You are a Protestant, so you will never understand it.
There is a woman nodding approval. I now
become aware of a bill posted on the wall of
the church. It reads as follows:

Soldiers!
When you feel that you are under the power of the Lord avoid talking directly to him. The Lord is not
accessible to words. We also recommend urgently that you should not
indulge in discussions about the at-
tributes of the Lord among your-
selves. It would be fruitless, as anything of value and importance is in-
effable.
Signed: Pope. . . . (the name,
however, is not decipherable)

We now enter the church. The interior
resembles a mosque rather than a church, as a
matter of fact it is particularly like the Hagia
Sophia. There are no chairs, which produces a
wonderful effect of space. There are also no

images. There are only framed sentences on
the walls (like those in the Hagia Sophia).
One of these sentences reads, "Do not flatter
your benefactor." The same woman who nod-
ded approval to me before begins to weep and
says, "I think that it is perfectly all right," but
she vanishes.

At first I am right in front of a pillar
which obliterates the view; then I change my
position and I see a crowd of people in front
of me. I do not belong to them, and I am
standing alone. But I see them clearly, and I
also see their faces. They pronounce the following words; "we confess that we are under
the power of the Lord. The Kingdom of
Heaven is within ourselves." They repeat this
thrice in a most solemn way. Then the organ
plays a fugue by Bach and a choir sings. Sometimes it is music alone, sometimes the following words are repeated: "Everything else is
paper," which means that it does not produce
a living impression.

When the music is finished the second
part of the ceremony begins, as is the custom
at students' meetings where the dealing with
serious affairs is followed by the gay part of
the gathering. There are serene and mature
human beings. One walks to and fro, others
talk together, they welcome each other, and
wine from the episcopal seminary and other
drinks are served. In the form of a toast one
wishes the church a favorable development,
and a radio amplifier plays a ragtime melody

with the refrain: "Charles is now also in the game." It is as if the pleasure concerning some new member of the society were to be expressed by that performance. A priest explains to me: "These somewhat futile amusements are officially acknowledged and admitted. We must adapt a little to American methods. If you have to deal with big crowds, as we have, it is inevitable. We differ, however, on principle from the American churches in that we cherish an emphatically anti-ascetic tendency." Whereupon I woke up with a feeling of great relief.[9]

In an attempt to interpret this dream Jung states his disagreement with Freud, who explains the dream as a mere façade behind which something has been carefully hidden. Jung says:

There is no doubt that neurotics hide disagreeable things, probably just as much as normal people do. But it is a serious question whether this category can be applied to such a normal and world-wide phenomenon as the dream. I am doubtful whether we can assume that a dream is something else than it appears to be. I am rather inclined to quote another Jewish authority, the Talmud, which says: "The dream is its own interpretation." In other words, I take the dream for granted. The dream is such a difficult and intricate subject that I do not dare to make any assumptions about its possible cunning. The dream

[9] *Ibid.*, p. 28 ff.

is a natural event, and there is no reason under the sun why we should assume that it is a crafty device to lead us astray. The dream occurs when consciousness and will are to a great extent extinguished. It seems to be a natural product which is also to be found in people who are not neurotic. Moreover, we know so little about the psychology of the dream process that we must be more than careful when we introduce elements foreign to the dream itself into its explanation.

For all these reasons I hold that our dream really speaks of religion and that it means to do so. Since the dream is elaborate and consistent it suggests a certain logic and a certain intention, that is, it is preceded by a motivation in the unconscious which finds direct expression in the dream content.[10]

What is Jung's interpretation of the dream? He remarks that the Catholic Church, though it is strongly recommended, appears to be coupled with a strange pagan point of view which is irreconcilable to a fundamentally Christian attitude; that there is no opposition to collective feeling, mass religion, and paganism in the whole dream of his patient except the soon-silenced Protestant friend. He explains the unknown woman in the dream as a representation of the "anima" which to him is the "psychical representation of the minority of female genes in a male body." The anima as a rule personifies the unconscious and gives it its purely disagreeable and irritating character.

[10] *Ibid.,* p. 31.

The wholly negative reaction of the anima to the church dream points out that the dreamer's feminine, that is, his unconscious, side disagrees with his attitude.

We gather, then, from the dream that the unconscious functioning of the dreamer's mind produces a pretty flat compromise between Catholicism and a pagan joie de vivre. The product of the unconscious is manifestly not expressing a point of view or a definite opinion; it is rather a dramatic exposition of an act of deliberation. It could be formulated perhaps in the following way: "Now what about this religious business? You are a Catholic, are you not? Is that not good enough? But asceticism—well, well, even the church has to adapt a little—movies, radio, spiritual five-o'clock tea and all that—why not some ecclesiastical wine and gay acquaintances?" [11]

But for some secret reason this awkward mystery woman, well known from many former dreams, seems to be deeply disappointed and quits.

Describing his patient, Jung states that he had come to him because of a very serious experience:

Being highly rationalistic and intellectual, he had found that his attitude of mind and his philosophy forsook him completely in the face of his neurosis and its demoralizing forces. He found nothing in his whole Weltanschauung that would help him to gain a sufficient control over himself. He therefore was

[1] *Ibid.,* pp. 35, 36.

very much in the situation of a man deserted
by his heretofore cherished convictions and
ideals. It is by no means an extraordinary case
that under such conditions a man should return to the religion of his childhood in the
hope of finding something helpful there. It
was, however, not a conscious attempt or a decision to revivify former religious beliefs. He
merely dreamed it; that is, his unconscious
produced a peculiar statement about his religion. It is just as if the spirit and the flesh,
the eternal enemies in Christian consciousness, had made peace with each other in the
form of a curious mitigation of their contra-
dictory nature. Spirituality and worldliness
come together in unexpected peacefulness.
The effect is somewhat grotesque and comical.
The inexorable severity of the spirit seems to
be undermined by an almost antique gaiety,
perfumed by wine and roses. The dream certainly describes a spiritual and worldly atmosphere that dulls the sharpness of a moral conflict and swallows up in oblivion all mental
pain and distress.[12]

From the dream and the description of the
dreamer given by Jung, this interpretation does not
seem warranted. Jung's interpretation remains on the
surface and does not take into account the underlying
psychic forces that have produced this dream. As I see
it, the dream is not at all a flat compromise between
worldliness and religion, but a bitter accusation against

[12] *Ibid.*, pp. 36, 37.

religion and at the same time a serious wish for spiritual independence. The church is described in terms of a theater, a business firm, an army. Mohammedanism, represented by the Hagia Sophia, is favorably compared with the Christian Church because it has no images and only framed sentences like: "Do not flatter your benefactor." This sentence is, of course, the dreamer's own criticism against the church's habit of flattering God. The dreamer goes on making fun of the church by dreaming that the church service degenerates into a hilarious gathering in which drinks are served and a ragtime melody with the refrain "Charles is now also in the game" is played. (It seems to have escaped Jung's attention that the verse "Charles is now also in the game" has a reference to his own first name Carl [Charles], that this mocking remark at the analyst is in line with the spirit of rebellion against authority that pervades the whole dream.) The dreamer emphasizes this point by having the priest himself admit that the church must use "American methods" in order to attract big crowds.

The role of the woman in this dream can be fully understood only if we consider the anti-authoritarian, rebellious tendency of the whole dream. The dreamer —in spite of his conscious indifference to religion—is, on a deeper psychic level, still bound to it or rather, more accurately, to the authoritarian type of religion that was presented to him in his childhood. His neurosis is an attempt to free himself from the bondage to irrational authorities, but so far he has failed and as a result has developed neurotic patterns. In the period in which this dream occurs the attempt to rebel, to free himself from domination by authorities, is a dominant psychic trait which makes its appearance in his dream life. The woman, probably symbolizing his mother, realizes that if he repudiates the authoritarian principle of flattering the strong father figure (the benefactor) he will grow up and she will lose him, too. That is why she weeps and says, "Then there is nothing left at all."

The dreamer is indeed concerned with religion but not, as Jung assumes, arriving at a flat compromise but at a very clear concept of the difference between authoritarian and humanistic religion. Authoritarian religion, a system in which obedience is the basic virtue and man makes himself small and powerless, giving all power and strength to God, is the type of religion he fights against; this battle is the same which pervades his personal life, the rebellion against any kind of authoritarian domination. What he is striving for is humanistic religion, where the emphasis is on man's strength and goodness and where virtue is not obedience but the realization of one's human powers.[13] The sequence of the dream makes this very clear. He hears the crowd "in a most solemn way" pronounce the words, "The kingdom of heaven is within ourselves . . . Everything else is paper." The dreamer has derided the church as a big organization like a business firm or the army, he has accused it of using flattery to win God's favors, and he is saying now that God lives within our-

---

[13] Cf. the discussion of authoritarian and humanistic religion in E. Fromm, *Psychoanalysis and Religion* (New Haven: Yale University Press, 1950).

selves and that aside from this experience "everything else is paper" because it does not produce a living impression.

The same trend of thought appears in the second dream of the same patient which Jung discusses in *Psychology and Religion*.[14]

This is the text of the dream:

> I am entering a solemn house. It is called "the house of inner composure or self collection." In the background are many burning candles arranged so as to form four pyramid-like points. An old man stands at the door of the house. People enter, they do not talk and often stand still in order to concentrate. The old man at the door tells me about the visitors to the house and says: "When they leave they are pure." I enter the house now, and I am able to concentrate completely: A voice says: "What thou art doing is dangerous. Religion is not a tax which thou payest in order to get rid of the woman's image for this image is indispensable. Woe to those who use religion as a substitute for the other side of the soul's life. They are in error and they shall be cursed. Religion is no substitute, but it is the ultimate accomplishment added to every other activity of the soul. Out of the fullness of life thou shalt give birth to thy religion and only then shalt thou be blessed." Together with the last sentence a faint music becomes audible, simple tunes played by an organ, reminding me

[14] *Ibid.*, pp. 42, 43.

somewhat of Wagner's "Fire magic" (Feuer-
zauber). As I leave the house I have the vision
of a flaming mountain and I feel that a fire
which can not be quenched must be a sacred
fire.

In this dream the dreamer is no longer attacking
the church in the facetious way of his previous dream.
He makes a profound and clear statement about humanistic religion as against authoritarian religion. He emphasizes particularly one point: religion must not try to
suppress love and sex (the woman's image) and must
not be a substitute for this side of life. Not out of sup-
pression but out of "the fullness of life" must religion be
born. The last statement of the dream "that a fire which
can not be quenched must be a sacred fire" refers, as is
clear from the whole context of the dream, to what is
expressed by the "image of the woman," the fire of love
and of sex.

This dream is interesting as an illustration for that
kind of dream in which the mind expresses thoughts
and judgments with a clarity and beauty the dreamer
has not arrived at in his waking life. But I have
quoted it primarily in order to illustrate the shortcom-
ings of Jung's one-sided and dogmatic interpretation.
To him the "unquenchable fire" symbolizes God, the
"image of the woman" and "the other side of life" stand
for the unconscious. While it is perfectly true that fire is
a frequent symbol of God, it is often a symbol of love
and of sexual passion. Freud probably would have interpreted the dream as expressing not a philosophical
statement but as the wish-fulfillment of the dreamer's

infantile, incestuous wishes. Jung, equally dogmatically, ignores this aspect completely and thinks only of religious symbolism. The truth seems to me to lie in neither of these two directions. The dreamer is indeed concerned with a religious and a philosophical problem, but he does not separate his philosophical concern from his own longing for love. On the contrary, he states that they must not be separated, and he criticizes the Church for her concept of sin.

V

The History of

Dream Interpretation

THREE APPROACHES TO THE UNDERSTANDING OF DREAMS
have been presented so far. First, the Freudian view,
which says that all dreams are expressions of the irrational and asocial nature of man. Second, Jung's interpretation, which says that dreams are revelations of unconscious wisdom, transcending the individual. Third,
the view that dreams express any kind of mental activity
and are expressive of our irrational strivings as well as
of our reason and morality, that they express both the
worst and the best in ourselves.

These three theories are by no means of recent
date. A brief survey of the history of dream interpretation shows that the recent controversy about the meaning of dreams contains a discussion which has been going on for at least the past three thousand years.

1. Early Nonpsychological Interpretation of Dreams

The history of dream interpretation begins with attempts to understand the meaning of dreams, not as
psychological phenomena but as real experiences of the

disembodied soul or as the voice of spirits or ghosts. Thus the Ashanti assume that, if a man dreams of having sexual intercourse with another man's wife, he will be fined the usual adultery fee, for his soul and hers have had sexual intercourse.[1] The Kiwai Papuans of British New Guinea believe that if a sorcerer manages to catch the soul of somebody in the state of dreaming, the sleeper will never wake up.[2] Another form of the belief that the occurrences of the dream are real is the idea that spirits of departed men appear in the dream to exhort us, warn us, or give us other kinds of messages. With the Mohave and Yuma Indians, for instance, the appearance of recently dead relatives in dreams is particularly dreaded.[3] Another concept of the meaning of dreams, closer to the one also to be found in the great cultures of the East, is held by other primitive peoples. Here, the dream is interpreted in a fixed religious and moral frame of reference. Each symbol has its definite meaning, and interpreting the dream consists of translating these fixed symbolic meanings. An example of this kind of interpretation is related by Jackson S. Lincoln in his study of the Navaho Indians:[4]

> The Dream: I dreamed of a very large
> egg made of a hard rocky substance. I cracked

[1] R. S. Rattray, "Religion and Art in the Ashanti." Quoted from R. Wood, *World of Dreams,* an Anthology, Random House, New York, 1947.
[2] Gunnar Landtman, "The Kiwai Papuans of British New Guinea." Quoted from Wood, *op. cit.*
[3] E. W. Gifford, "Mohave and Yuma Indians," *Journal of American Folklore,* January-March, 1926. Quoted from Wood, *op. cit.*
[4] Jackson S. Lincoln, "The Dream in Primitive Culture." Quoted from Wood, *op. cit.*

open the egg and out flew a young but full-grown eagle. It was indoors, and the eagle flew all around trying to fly out, but it could not get out because the window was shut.

The Interpretation: The eagle belongs to the bird group of the higher spirits which is one of a group of three allied spirits, namely, the wind, the lightning and the birds, all of which live on the top of San Francisco mountain. These spirits can wreak great havoc and destruction if offended. They can also be friendly. The eagle cannot fly out because you must have offended the bird spirit, possibly by walking on its nest, or perhaps your father has committed the offense.

Early Oriental dream interpretation also was not based on a psychological theory of dreams but on the assumption that the dream was a message sent to men by divine powers. The best-known examples of this type of nonpsychological dream interpretation are Pharaoh's dreams reported in the Bible. When Pharaoh had a dream which troubled his spirit, "he sent and called for all the magicians of Egypt and all the wise men thereof: and Pharaoh told them his dream; but there was none that could interpret them unto Pharaoh." When he requests Joseph to interpret the dream, Joseph answers, "God has shown Pharaoh what he is about to do." And then he proceeds to interpret the dream. The dream was:

Pharaoh dreamed; and, behold he stood by the river. And, behold, there came up out of the river seven well-favoured kine and fat-fleshed; and they fed in a meadow. And, behold, seven other kine came up after them out of the river, ill-favoured and lean-fleshed; and stood by the other kine upon the brink of the river. And the ill-favoured and lean-fleshed kine did eat up the seven well-favoured and fat kine. So Pharaoh awoke. And he slept and dreamed the second time: and, behold, seven ears of corn came up upon one stalk, rank and good. And, behold, seven thin ears and blasted with the east wind sprung up after them. And the seven thin ears devoured the seven rank and full ears. And Pharaoh awoke, and, behold, it was a dream.

Joseph's interpretation is:

The seven good kine are seven years; and the seven good ears are seven years: the dream is one. And the seven thin and ill-favoured kine that came up after them are seven years; and the seven empty ears blasted with the east wind shall be seven years of famine. This is the thing which I have spoken unto Pharaoh: What God is about to do he sheweth unto Pharaoh. Behold, there come seven years of great plenty throughout all the land of Egypt: and there shall arise after them seven years of famine; and all the plenty shall be forgotten in the land of Egypt; and the famine shall consume the land; and the plenty shall not be known in the land by reason of that famine following; for it shall be very grievous. And

for that the dream was doubled unto Pharaoh
twice; it is because the thing is established by
God, and God will shortly bring it to pass.
Now therefore let Pharaoh look out a man
discreet and wise, and set him over the land
of Egypt. Let Pharaoh do this, and let him appoint officers over the land, and take up the
fifth part of the land of Egypt in the seven
plenteous years. And let them gather all the
food of those good years that come, and lay up
corn under the hand of Pharaoh, and let them
keep food in the cities. And that food shall be
for store to the land against the seven years of
famine, which shall be in the land of Egypt;
that the land perish not through the famine.

The Biblical report says that the dream was looked
upon as the vision shown to man by God. However, it
is possible to look at Pharaoh's dream from a psychological viewpoint. He could have known certain factors
which would influence the conditions of the fertility of
the soil in the coming fourteen years, but this intuitive
knowledge might have been available to him only under the condition of sleep. Whether the dream is to be
understood in this way or not is a matter of speculation;
at any rate, the Biblical report, like many other reports
from old Oriental sources, shows that the dream was
understood not as something coming from man but as
a divine message.

Dreams were supposed to have another kind of predictive function, particularly in Indian and Greek
dream interpretation: that of diagnosing illness. Fixed

symbols were used to denote certain somatic symptoms. But here, too, as in Pharaoh's predictive dream, a psychological interpretation is possible. We can assume that in our sleep we have a much finer awareness of certain bodily changes than we have in our waking life, and that this awareness is translated into the image of a dream and thus can serve to diagnose illness and predict certain somatic occurrences. (The extent to which this is so would have to be demonstrated by the extensive study of dreams of people before the manifest occurrence of illness.)

2. *The Psychological Interpretation of Dreams*

In contrast to the nonpsychological interpretation of dreams, which takes the dream as the expression of "real" occurrences or as messages from powers outside of man, the psychological interpretation of dreams tries to understand the dream as an expression of the dreamer's own mind. These two approaches are by no means always separate. On the contrary, until the Middle Ages we find many authors who combine both viewpoints and differentiate between dreams which must be interpreted as religious phenomena and those dreams which need to be understood psychologically. One illustration of this kind of approach is expressed by an Indian author at about the beginning of the Christian era:

> There are six kinds of people who see dreams—the man who is of a windy humor, or of a bilious one, or of a phlegmatic one, the man who dreams dreams by the influence of a

god, the man who does so by the influence of his own habits, and the man who does so in the way of prognostication. And of those, O king, only the last kind of dreams is true; all the rest are false.[5]

In contrast to the nonpsychological interpretation, in which a dream is understood by translating its fixed symbols from their religious context, our Indian source follows the method of all psychological dream interpretation—to relate the dream to the personality of the dreamer. His first three categories are really one, since they refer to temperament—those psychic qualities which are rooted in a constitutionally given somatic basis. He points to a significant connection between temperament and dream content which has hardly found any attention in contemporary dream interpretation, although it is a significant aspect of dream interpretation, as further research will undoubtedly show. To him, dreams sent by a god represent just one type of dream among others. He then differentiates between those dreams which are influenced by the habits of the dreamer and those which represent prognostication. By habits he probably means the dominant drives in a person's character structure; by prognostication, to those dreams which are the expression of superior insight during sleep.

One of the earliest expressions of the view that dreams can be the expression of either our most rational or our most irrational powers is found in Homer.

[5] "The Questions of King Milinda" (unknown authorship, written in Northern India about the beginning of the Christian era). Translated by T. W. Rhys David. Quoted from Wood, *op. cit.*

He assigns two gates to dreams: the horny one of truth, the ivory one of error and delusion (referring to the transparent qualities of horn, whereas ivory is not transparent). The ambiguous nature of dream activity could hardly be expressed more clearly and concisely.

Socrates, as quoted in Plato's *Phaedo*, held the view that dreams represent the voice of conscience and that it is of the utmost importance to take this voice seriously and to follow it. In an incident shortly before his death, he makes this position very clear:

> Cebes said: I am glad, Socrates, that you mentioned the name of Aesop. For it reminds me of a question which has been asked by many, and was asked of me only the day before yesterday by Evenus the poet; he will be sure to ask it again, and therefore if you would like me to have an answer ready for him you may as well tell me what I should say to him; He wanted to know why you, who never before wrote a line of poetry, now that you are in prison are putting Aesop's fables into verse, and also composing that hymn in honor of Apollo.
>
> Tell him, Cebes, he replied, what is the truth, that I had no idea of rivaling him or his poems; to do so, as I knew would be no easy task. But I wanted to see whether I could purge away a scruple which I felt about the meaning of certain dreams. In the course of my life I have often had intimations in dreams that I should compose music. The same dream came to me sometimes in one

form, and sometimes in another, but always saying the same or nearly the same words: "Make and cultivate music," said the dream. And hitherto I had imagined that this was only intended to exhort and encourage me in the study of philosophy, which has always been the pursuit of my life, and is the noblest and best of music. The dream was bidding me to do what I was already doing, in the same way that the competitor in a race is bidden by the spectators to run when he is already running. But I was not certain of this; for the dream might have meant music in the popular sense of the word, and being under sentence of death, and the festival giving me a respite, I thought that it would be safer for me to satisfy the scruple, and, in obedience to the dream, to compose a few verses before I departed. And first I made a hymn in honor of the god of the festival, and then considering that a poet, if he is really to be a poet, should not only put together words but should invent stories, and that I have no invention, I took some fables of Aesop, which I had ready at hand and knew—they were the first I came upon—and turned them into verse. Tell this to Evenus, Cebes, and bid him be of good cheer; say that I would have him come after me if he be a wise man, and not tarry; and that today I am likely to be going, for the Athenians say that I must." [6]

[6] Plato, Phaedo. Translated by B. Jowett. Published for the Classics Club by Walter J. Black, 1943, New York. pp. 88, 89.

Quite in contrast to Socrates's view, Plato's theory of dreams is an almost literal anticipation of Freud's dream theory.

> . . . Certain of the unnecessary pleasures and appetites I conceive to be unlawful; every one appears to have them, but in some persons they are controlled by the laws and by reason, and the better desires prevail over them— either they are wholly banished or they become few and weak; while in the case of others they are stronger, and there are more of them.
>
> Which appetites do you mean?
>
> I mean those which are awake when the reasoning and human and ruling power is asleep; . . . and there is no conceivable folly or crime—not excepting incest or any other unnatural union, or parricide, or the eating of forbidden food—which at such a time, when he has parted company with all shame and sense, a man may not be ready to commit.
>
> Most true, he said.
>
> But when a man's pulse is healthy and temperate, and when before going to sleep he has awakened his rational powers, and fed them on noble thoughts and enquiries, collecting himself in meditation; after having first indulged his appetites neither too much nor too little, but just enough to lay them to sleep, and prevent them and their enjoyments and pains from interfering with the higher principle—which he leaves in the solitude of pure

abstraction, free to contemplate and aspire to the knowledge of the unknown, whether in past, present or future: when again he has allayed the passionate element, if he has a quarrel against any one—I say, when, after pacifying the two irrational principles, he rouses up the third, which is reason, before he takes his rest, then, as you know, he attains truth most nearly, and is least likely to be the sport of fantastic and lawless visions.

I quite agree.

In saying this I have been running into a digression; but the point which I desire to note is that in all of us, even in good men, there is a lawless wild-beast nature, which peers out in sleep. Pray, consider whether I am right, and you agree with me.

Yes, I agree.[7]

While Plato, like Freud, looks at dreams as the expression of the irrational animal in us, he makes one qualification which restricts this interpretation to some extent. He assumes that if the sleeper falls asleep in a mood of quiet and inner peace, his dreams will be least irrational. This view, however, must not be confused with the dualistic interpretation that dreams are the expression of both our irrational and our rational nature; to Plato they are essentially the expression of the savage and terrible in us and only less so in the person who has achieved the greatest maturity and wisdom.

[7] Plato's *The Republic*. Translated into English by B. Jowett, M.A. (The Modern Library, New York, Random House), pp. 330, 331.

Aristotle's view on dreams stresses their rational nature. He assumes that during our sleep we are capable of more refined observations of subtle bodily occurrences and furthermore that we are occupied with plans and principles of action and visualize those more clearly than in the daytime. He does not assume, however, that all dreams are meaningful but that many are accidents and do not deserve to be credited with predictive functions. The following passage from *On Divination* shows his position:

> . . . Well then, the dreams in question must be regarded either as *causes,* or as *tokens,* of the events, or else as *coincidences;* either as all, or some, of these, or as one only. I use the word "cause" in the sense in which the moon is [the cause] of an eclipse of the sun, or in which fatigue is [a cause] of fever; "token" [in the sense in which] the entrance of a star [into the shadow] is a token of the eclipse, or [in which] roughness of the tongue [is a token] of fever; while by "coincidence" I mean, for example, the occurrence of an eclipse of the sun while some one is taking a walk; for the walking is neither a token nor a cause of the eclipse, nor the eclipse [a cause or token] of the walking. For this reason no coincidence takes place according to a universal or general rule. Are we then to say that some dreams are causes, other tokens, e.g. of events taking place in the bodily organism? At all events, even scientific physicians tell us that one should pay diligent attention to dreams,

and to hold this view is reasonable also for
those who are not practitioners, but specula-
tive philosophers. For the movements which
occur in the daytime [within the body] are,
unless very great and violent, lost sight of in
contrast with the waking movements, which
are more impressive. In sleep the opposite
takes place, for then even trifling movements
seem considerable. This is plain in what often
happens during sleep; for example, dreamers
fancy that they are affected by thunder and
lightning, when in fact there are only faint
ringings in their ears; or that they are enjoy-
ing honey or other sweet savours, when only a
tiny drop of phlegm is flowing down [the
oesophagus]; or that they are walking through
fire, and feeling intense heat, when there is
only a slight warmth affecting certain parts of
the body. When they are awakened, these
things appear to them in this their true character. But since the beginnings of all events
are small, so, it is clear, are those also of the
diseases or other affections about to occur in
our bodies. In conclusion, it is manifest that
these beginnings must be more evident in
sleeping than in waking moments.

Nay, indeed, it is not improbable that
some of the presentations which come before
the mind in sleep may even be causes of the
actions cognate to each of them. For as when
we are about to act [in waking hours], or are
engaged in any course of action, or have already performed certain actions, we often find

ourselves concerned with these actions, or performing them, in a vivid dream; the cause whereof is that the dream-movement has had a way paved for it from the original movements set up in the daytime; exactly so, but conversely, it must happen that the movements set up first in sleep should also prove to be starting-points of actions to be performed in the daytime, since the recurrence by day of the thought of these actions also has had its way paved for it in the images before the mind at night. Thus then it is quite conceivable that some dreams may be tokens and causes [of future events].

Most [so-called prophetic] dreams are, however, to be classed as mere coincidences, especially all such as are extravagant, and those in the fulfilment of which the dreamers have no initiative, such as in the case of a sea-fight, or of things taking place far away. As regards these it is natural that the fact should stand as it does whenever a person, on mentioning something, finds the very thing mentioned come to pass. Why, indeed, should this not happen also in sleep? The probability is, rather, that many such things should happen. As, then, one's mentioning a particular person is neither token nor cause of this person's presenting himself, so, in the parallel instance, the dream is, to him who has seen it, neither token nor cause of its [so-called] fulfilment, but a mere coincidence. Hence the fact that many dreams have no "fulfilment," for coin-

cidences do not occur according to any universal or general law.[8]

Roman dream theory follows pretty much the principles developed in Greece but it does not always attain
the clarity and depth of insight that we find with Plato
and Aristotle. Lucretius, in *De Rerum Natura,* comes
close to Freud's theory of wish-fulfillment although
without Freud's emphasis on the irrational nature of
these wishes. He states that our dreams deal with things
we are interested in during the daytime or with bodily
needs which are satisfied in the dream:

> And whatever be the pursuit to which
> one clings with devotion, whatever the things
> on which we have been occupied much in the
> past, the mind being thus more intent upon
> that pursuit, it is generally the same things
> that we seem to encounter in dreams: pleaders
> to plead their cause and collate laws, gen-
> erals to contend and engage battle, sailors to
> fight out their war already begun with the
> winds, I myself to ply my own task, always
> seeking the nature of things and when found
> setting it forth in our own language. Thus too
> all other pursuits and arts usually seem in
> sleep to hold fast men's minds with their de-
> lusions. And whenever men have given con-
> stant attention to the games through many
> days on end, we usually see that when they

[8] *The Works of Aristotle.* Translated into English under the editorship
of W. D. Ross, M.A., Hon. LL.D. (Edin.) Volume III, The Parva
Naturalia, by J. I. Beare, M.A., De Divinatione Per Somnum, Chapter
I, Oxford, At The Clarendon Press, 1908.

have now ceased to observe all this with their senses, yet certain passages are left open in the mind by which the images of these things can come in. For many days then these same things are moving before their eyes, so that even while awake they seem to perceive dancers swaying their supple limbs, to hear in their ears the lyre's rippling tune and its speaking strings, to behold the same assemblage and with it the diverse glories of the stage in their brightness. Of so great import are devotion and pleasure, and what those things are which not men only but indeed all creatures are in the habit of practising.[9]

The most systematic theory of dream interpretation is given by Artemidorus in the second century A.D. in his book on the interpretation of dreams, a work which had great influence on medieval views. According to him, there are five kinds of dreams that have different qualities:

The first is a Dream: the second a Vision: the third an Oracle: the fourth a Phantasy or vain Imagination: the fifth an Apparition.
That is called a Dream which discovers the truth under a hidden figure; as when Joseph interpreted Pharaoh's Dream of the seven lean kine that should devour the seven fat ones, and the same of the ears of corn, etc.
A Vision is this: When a man really sees

[9] Reprinted by permission of the publishers from the Loeb Classical Library edition of LUCRETIUS—De Rerum Natura, translated by W. H. D. Rouse (Cambridge, Mass.: Harvard University Press, 1924). pp. 317, 318.

awake, what he did asleep; as it happened to
Vespatian, when he saw the Surgeon that
drew out Hero's tooth.

An Oracle is a revelation or advertise-
ment made to us in our sleep by some Angel,
or other Saint, to perform God's will according to their information; as it happened to
Joseph, the husband of the Holy Virgin, and
the Three Wise Men.

The Phantasy, or vain Imagination, happens in that instant when the affections are so
vehement that they ascend up to the brain
during our sleep, and meet with the more
watchful spirits; thus what the thoughts are
employed about in the day, we fancy in the
night; so a lover, who in the daytime thinks
on his fair one, in the night when asleep meets
with the same thoughts. It happens also, that
he that fasts all day, dreams at night that he is
feeding; or if thirsty in the daytime, in the
nighttime he dreams of drinking, and is very
much delighted with it. And the miser and
userer dreams of bags of money, nay will dis-
course of them in their sleep.

An Apparition is no other than a noc-
turnal Vision that presents itself to weak infants and ancient men, who fancy they see
chimeras approaching to intimidate or offend
them.[10]

We see that Artemidorus assumes what he calls a
"dream" to be an insight expressed in symbolic language. To him, Pharaoh's dream is not a vision sent to

[10] Quoted from Wood, *op. cit.*

him by God but the symbolic expression of his own rational insight. He holds that there are dreams in which an angel reveals God's will to us but to these he gives the name "oracle." The dream that is the expression of our irrational desires is recognized by him as one of the various kinds of dreams, and he calls that dream to which Flato and Freud's interpretation applies the fantasy, or vain Imagination. Anxiety dreams, called apparitions, are explained as caused by the peculiar conditions of weak infants and old men. Artemidorus states explicitly the significant principle that "the rules of dreaming are not general, and therefore cannot satisfy all persons, seeing they often, according to times and persons, admit of varied interpretations."

Our picture of Roman dream interpretation would be incomplete without hearing the voice of complete skepticism, that of Cicero. In his poem *On Divination* he writes:

> Dreams are not entitled to any credit or respect whatever.
>
> If, then, dreams do not come from God, and if there are no objects in nature with which they have a necessary sympathy and connection, and if it is impossible by experiments and observations to arrive at a sure interpretation of them, the consequence is that dreams are not entitled to any credit or respect whatever. . . .
>
> Let us reject, therefore, this divination of dreams, as well as all other kinds. For, to speak truly, that superstition has extended it-

self through all nations, and has oppressed the intellectual energies of all men, and has betrayed them into endless imbecilities.[11]

Dating back to about the same time an elaborate theory of dreams is reported in the Talmud. The role that dream interpretation played in Jerusalem around the time of Christ can be recognized from the statement in the Talmud[12] that there were twenty-four dream interpreters in Jerusalem. Rabbi Chisda said: "Each dream has meaning except one which is stimulated by fasting. Furthermore, the dream which is not interpreted is like a letter which is not read." This statement formulates the principles that Freud announced in similar words almost two thousand years later: that all dreams without exception are meaningful and that dreams are important communications to ourselves, the interpretation of which we cannot afford to ignore. Rabbi Chisda adds a significant qualification to the general principle of the psychological interpretation of dreams by pointing to those caused by fasting. In more general terms, his qualification is that those dreams which are caused by strong physical somatic stimuli are the one exception to the general rule of psychic determinism in dreams.

The Talmudic authors assumed that certain types of dreams were predictive. Rabbi Jochanan said, "Three kinds of dreams come true: the dream in the morning, the dream which someone has about one, and the dream which is interpreted by another dream. According to

[11] Quoted from Wood, *op. cit.*
[12] Berachoth, 55a.

others, the repetitive dream also is among those which come true." [13]

Although no reasons are given for this assumption, they are not too difficult to discover. The sleep in the morning is less deep than that in the early night, and the sleeper is closer to his waking consciousness. Rabbi Jochanan apparently assumes that in this state of sleep rational judgment enters into the dream process and permits us to have clearer insight into forces operating in us or in others, and thus to predict events. The assumption that a dream which someone else has about us comes true seems to be based on the idea that others often have better judgment about us than we have ourselves, and that in the state of sleep their insight into us is particularly sharp and therefore has predictive value. The reasoning behind the theory about that dream coming true which is interpreted by another dream is probably that, in the state of sleep, we are capable of intuitive insight which permits us to interpret a dream by dreaming its "interpretation." Recent experiments with dream interpretation under hypnosis seem to confirm this view. People put under hypnosis and asked to interpret various dreams gave without hesitation a meaningful interpretation of the symbolic language employed by the dream. When not under hypnosis, the same dream seemed to them completely meaningless. These experiments tend to show that we all possess the gift to understand symbolic language, but that this knowledge becomes operative only in the state of disassociation brought about by hypnosis. Our Tal-

[13] *Ibid.*, 55b.

mudic author holds that the same holds true for the
state of sleep, that when asleep we understand the
meaning of another dream and can interpret it correctly.
There is little doubt that the repetitive dream has a
particular significance. Many contemporary psycholo-
gists observe that a dream which a person has repeated-
ly is expressive of the important themes of his life. Inasmuch as a person tends to act again and again according to such a *leitmotif*, it may be said that such repeated
dreams also often predict future events in the person's
life.

Of particular interest is the Talmudic interpretation
of symbols. It follows Freudian lines as, for instance, in
the interpretation of a dream that someone "waters an
olive tree with olive oil." [14] The interpretation is that
this dream symbolizes incest. In a dream where the
dreamer sees his eyes kissing each other, the symbol
means sexual intercourse with his sister. But while
symbols not sexual in themselves are interpreted as having sexual meaning, symbols directly sexual are interpreted as meaning something nonsexual. Thus our Talmudic source says that the dream in which someone
has intercourse with his mother means that he can hope
to have a great deal of wisdom. Or that one who dreams
that he had sexual relations with a married woman
can be sure of his own salvation. The Talmudic interpretation is apparently based on the idea that a symbol
always stands for something else and, therefore, a symbol which in itself is sexual must mean something different from its manifest meaning. However, an interesting

[14] *Ibid.*, 56b.

qualification is made. The man who dreams about intercourse with a married woman can be sure of his salvation only if he has not known the woman of his dream before, and if he had no sexual desire when he fell asleep.[15] We see here how much importance the Talmudic view gives to the state of mind of the dreamer before he fell asleep. If he had sexual desires or even if he had known only casually the woman about whom he has the dream, we must expect that the general rule that a symbol stands for something else is not valid and that the sexual symbolism is expressive of a sexual wish.

Medieval dream interpretation follows pretty much the line we have seen in classic antiquity. An author of the fourth century, Synesius of Cyrene, makes one of the most precise and beautiful statements of the theory that dreams stem from the heightened capacity of insight during sleep.[16]

> If dreams prophesy the future, if visions which present themselves to the mind during sleep afford some *indicia* whereby to divine future things—dreams will be at the same time true and obscure, and even in their obscurity the truth will reside. "The gods with a thick veil have covered human life." [Hesiod]
>
> I am not surprised that some have owed to a sleep the discovery of a treasure; and that one may have gone to sleep very ignorant, and after having had in a dream a conversation with the Muses, awakened an able poet,

[15] *Ibid.*, 56b.
[16] Synesius of Cyrene: *On Dreams*, translated by Isaac Myer. Quoted from Wood, *op. cit.*

which has happened in my time to some, and
in which there is nothing strange. I do not
speak of those who have had, in their sleep,
the revelation of a danger which threatened
them, or the knowledge of a remedy that
would cure them. But when sleep opens the
way to the most perfect inspections of true
things to the soul which previously had not
desired these inspections, nor thought concerning the ascent to intellect and arouses it
to pass beyond nature and reunite itself to the
intelligible sphere from which it has wan-
dered so far that it does not know even from
whence it came, *this*, I say, is most marvelous
and obscure.

If one thinks it extraordinary that the
soul may thus ascend to the superior region,
and does not believe that the way to this felici-
tous union lies through the imagination let
him hear the sacred oracles when they speak
about the different roads which lead to the
higher sphere. After enumerating the various
subsidia which help the ascent of the soul by
arousing and developing its powers, they say:

> By lessons some are enlightened,
> By sleep others are inspired.

Sibylline Oracles

You see the distinction which the oracle
establishes: upon the one side, inspiration;
upon the other, study; the former, it says, is
instruction whilst one is awake, the latter
when asleep. Whilst awake, it is always a
man who is the instructor: but when asleep,

it is from God that the knowledge comes. . . .

Thanks to its character, divination by dreams is placed within the reach of all: plain and without artifice, it is pre-eminently rational; holy, because it does not make use of violent methods, it can be exercised anywhere: it dispenses with fountain, rock and gulf, and it thus is that which is truly divine. To practice it there is no need of neglecting any of our occupations, or to rob our business for a single moment. . . . No one is advised to quit his work and go to sleep, especially to have dreams. But as the body cannot resist prolonged night-watches, the time that nature has ordained for us to consecrate to repose brings us, with sleep, an accessory more precious than sleep itself: that natural necessity becomes a source of enjoyment and we do not sleep merely to live, but to learn to live well. . . .

But in divination by dreams, each of us is in himself his proper instrument; whatever we may do, we cannot separate ourselves from our oracle: it dwells with us; it follows us everywhere, in our journeys, in war, in public life, agricultural pursuits, in commercial enterprises. The laws of a jealous Republic do not interdict that divination; if they did they could do nothing: because how can the offense be proven. What harm is there in sleeping? No tyrant is able to carry out an edict against dreams, still less proscribe sleep in his dominions; that would be at once folly to command the impossible, and an impiety to put himself in opposition to the desires of nature and God.

Then let us all deliver ourselves to the interpretation of dreams, men and women, young and old, rich and poor, private citizens and magistrates, inhabitants of the town and of the country, artisans and orators. There is not any privileged, neither by sex, neither by age, nor fortune or profession. Sleep offers itself to all: it is an oracle always ready to be our infallible and silent counselor; in these mysteries of a new species each is at the same time priest and initiate. It, as well as divination, announces to us the joys to come, and through the anticipated happiness which it procures for us, it gives to our pleasures a longer duration; and it warns us to the misfortunes that threaten us, so that we may be put on our guard. The charming promises of hope so dear to man, the farseeing calculations of fear, all come to us through dreams. Nothing is more qualified in its effect to nourish hope in us; this good, so great and so precious that without it we could not be able, as said the most illustrious Sophists, to support life. . . .

Similar to the point of view held by Synesius are the dream theories of the Jewish Aristotelians in the twelfth and thirteenth centuries. The greatest of them, Maimonides, states that dreams, like prophecy, are due to the action of the imaginative faculty during sleep. Whether the dreamer himself is able to separate the rational part of the dream from its symbolic veil or whether he needs the help of a dream interpreter depends on the degree to which the insight is veiled in symbols and on the strength of his reasoning power.[17]

Thomas Aquinas differentiates between four kinds of dreams:

> As stated above divination is superstitious and unlawful when it is based on a false opinion. Wherefore we must consider what is true in the matter of foreknowing the future from dreams. Now dreams are sometimes the cause of future occurrences; for instance, when a person's mind becomes anxious through what it has seen in a dream and is thereby led to do something or avoid something: while sometimes dreams are signs of future happenings, in so far as they are referable to some common cause of both dreams and future occurrences, and in this way the future is frequently known from dreams. We must, then, consider what is the cause of dreams, and whether it can be the cause of future occurrences, or be cognisant of them.
>
> Accordingly it is to be observed that the cause of dreams is sometimes in us and sometimes outside us. The inward cause of dreams is twofold: one regards the soul, in so far as those things which have occupied a man's thoughts and affections while awake recur to his imagination while asleep. A suchlike cause of dreams is not a cause of future occurrences,

[17] Gutman, *Die Philosophie des Judentums* (Munich: S. Hefka, 1933), p. 401.

so that dreams of this kind are related accidentally to future occurrences, and if at any time they concur it will be by chance. But sometimes the inward cause of dreams regards the body: because the inward disposition of the body leads to the formation of a movement in the imagination consistent with that disposition; thus a man in whom there is abundance of cold humours dreams that he is in the water or snow: and for this reason physicians say that we should take note of dreams in order to discover internal dispositions.

In like manner the outward cause of dreams is twofold, corporal and spiritual. It is corporal in so far as the sleeper's imagination is affected either by the surrounding air, or through an impression of a heavenly body, so that certain images appear to the sleeper, in keeping with the disposition of the heavenly bodies. The spiritual cause is sometimes referable to God, Who reveals certain things to men in their dreams by the ministry of the angels, according to Num. xii. 6, *If there be among you a prophet of the Lord, I will appear to him in a vision, or I will speak to him in a dream.* Sometimes, however, it is due to the action of the demons that certain images appear to persons in their sleep, and by this means they, at times, reveal certain future things to those who have entered into an unlawful compact with them.

Accordingly we must say that there is **no** unlawful divination in making use of dreams for the foreknowledge of the future, so long as those dreams are due to divine revelation, or to some natural cause inward or outward, and so far as the efficacy of that cause extends. But it will be an unlawful and superstitious divination if it be caused by a revelation of the demons, with whom a compact has been made, whether explicit, through their being invoked for the purpose, or implicit, through the divination extending beyond its possible limits.

This suffices for the *Replies* to the *Objections*.[18]

Aquinas, like Artemidorus and others, believed that some dreams are sent by God. Those dreams which he interprets as stemming from the dreamer's soul are not understood, as Maimonides maintained, as being the expression of the highest rational faculty but as the dreamer's imagination occupied with the same wishes and interests as during the day. It is interesting that, like Indian and Greek thinkers, Aquinas holds that certain somatic processes are indicated by the symbols of the dream and that internal somatic dispositions can be recognized by dream interpretation.

Modern dream interpretation (since the seventeenth century) is essentially a variation on the theories of antiquity and those of the Middle Ages, although certain new trends of thought make their appearance.

[18] The "Summa Theologica" of St. Thomas Aquinas, Part II, (Second Part), Question 95, Article 6, Literally Translated by Fathers of the English Dominican Province (Burns Oates & Washbourne Ltd., London, 1922), pp. 205, 206. Published in the United States by Benziger Brothers, New York.

While the theory that dreams can be the expression of somatic dispositions had been held by several older authors, Hobbes assumes that all dreams are the result of somatic stimuli, a view widely held up to the present and often used as refutation against Freud:

> And seeing dreams are caused by the distemper of some of the inward parts of the body; divers distempers must needs cause different dreams. And hence it is, that lying cold breedeth dreams of fear, and raiseth the thought and image of some fearful object (the motion from the brain to the inner parts, and from the inner parts to the brain being reciprocal:) and that, as anger causeth heat in some parts of the body, when we are awake, so when we sleep, the overheating of the same parts causeth anger, and raiseth up in the brain the imagination of an enemy. In the same manner, as natural kindness, when we are awake, causeth desire, and desire makes heat in certain other parts of the body; so also too much heat in those parts, while we sleep, raiseth in the brain an imagination of some kindness shown. In sum, our dreams are the reverse of our waking imaginations; the motion when we are awake, beginning at one end; and when we dream, at another.[19]

It is not surprising to find that the philosophers of the Enlightenment were skeptical about all claims that dreams were sent by God or could be used for purposes of divination.

[19] Thomas Hobbes, *Leviathan* (London, George Routledge & Sons, Ltd.), p. 6.

Voltaire denounces the idea that dreams predict and prophesy as superstitious nonsense. But in spite of this view he holds that, while dreams often are the expression of somatic stimuli and of excesses "in the passions of the soul," we also often make use of our highest rational faculties during sleep:

> We must acknowledge with Petronius: quidquid luce, tenebris agit. I have known advocates who have pleaded in dreams, mathematicians who have sought to solve problems; and poets who have composed verses. I have made some myself, which are very passable. It is therefore incontestable that consecutive ideas occur in sleep, as well as when we are awake, which ideas as certainly come in spite of us. We think while sleeping, as we move in our beds, without our will having anything to do either in the motive or the thought. Your Father Malebranche is right in asserting that we are not able to give ourselves ideas. For why are we to be masters of them, when waking, more than during sleep? [20]

Kant's theory of dreams is similar to Voltaire's. He, too, believed that we have no visions and holy inspirations in dreams. The basis for dreams is "simply caused by disordered stomach." But he also states that:

> I rather suppose, that . . . ideas in sleep may be clearer and broader than even the clearest

---

[20] Voltaire, A Philosophical Dictionary—"Somnambulists and Dreamers." Translated by F. Fleming, Copyright by E. R. Dumont, Vol. VII, part i, pp. 2 and 9.

in the waking state. This is to be expected of such an active being as the soul when the external senses are so completely at rest. For man, at such times, is not sensible of his body. When he wakes up, his body is not associated with the ideas of his sleep, so that it cannot be a means of recalling this former state of thought to consciousness in such a way as to make it appear to belong to one and the same person. A confirmation of my idea of sound sleep is found in the activity of some who walk in their sleep, and who, in such a state, betray more intelligence than usual, although in waking up they do not remember anything.

Dreams, however, i.e., the ideas that one remembers on waking up, do not belong here. For then man does not wholly sleep; he perceives to a certain degree clearly and weaves the actions of his spirit into the impressions of the external senses. He therefore remembers them in part afterwards, but finds in them only wild and absurd chimeras, since ideas of phantasy and of external sensation are intermingled in them.[21]

Goethe too emphasizes our increased rational capacity during sleep. When Eckermann told him of a rather poetic dream he had, Goethe stated:

We see . . . that the muses visit you even in sleep, and indeed with particular favor; for you must confess that it would be difficult for

[21] Immanuel Kant, *Dreams of a Spirit Seer.* Translated by E. F. Goerwitz (The Macmillan Co., New York, 1900).

you to invent anything so peculiar and pretty
in your waking moments.[22]

Not only is our power of imagination greater in our
sleep than in our waking life, but the innate strivings
for health and happiness often assert themselves in our
sleep more forcefully than when we are awake:

> Human nature possesses wonderful pow-
> ers, and has something good in readiness for
> us when we least hope for it. There have been
> times in my life when I have fallen asleep in
> tears; but in my dreams the most charming
> forms have come to console and to cheer me,
> and I have risen the next morning fresh and
> joyful.[22]

One of the most beautiful and concise statements
on the superior rational character of our mental process in sleep is made by Emerson:

> Dreams have a poetic integrity and truth.
> This limbo and dust-hole of thought is pre-
> sided over by a certain reason, too. Their ex-
> travagance from nature is yet within a higher
> nature. They seem to us to suggest an abun-
> dance and fluency of thought not familiar to
> the waking experience. They pique us by in-
> dependence of us, yet we know ourselves in
> this mad crowd, and owe to dreams a kind of
> divination and wisdom. My dreams are not
> me; they are not Nature, or the Not-me; they

[22] Goethe's conversation with Eckermann, translated by John Oxen-
fort, George Bell & Sons, New York, London, 1898, p. 315.

are both. They have a double consciousness,
at once sub- and ob-jective. We call the phan-
toms that rise, the creation of our fancy, but
they act like mutineers, and fire on their com-
mander; showing that every act, every
thought, every cause, is bipolar, and in the act
is contained the counteraction. If I strike, I am
struck; if I chase, I am pursued.

Wise and sometimes terrible hints shall
in them be thrown to the man out of a quite
unknown intelligence. He shall be startled
two or three times in his life by the justice as
well as the significance of this phantasmago-
ria. Once or twice the conscious fetters shall
seem to be unlocked, and a freer utterance attained. A prophetic character in all ages has
haunted them. They are the maturation often
of opinions not consciously carried out to
statements, but whereof we already possessed
the elements. Thus, when awake, I know the
character of Rupert, but do not think what he
may do. In dreams I see him engaged in certain actions which seem preposterous, out of
all fitness. He is hostile, he is cruel, he is
frightful, he is a poltroon. It turns out prophecy a year later. But it was already in my
mind as character, and the sibyl dreams
merely embodied it in fact. Why then should
not symptoms, auguries, forebodings be, as
one said, the meanings of the spirit?

We are led by this experience into the
high region of Cause and acquainted with the
identity of every unlikeseeming effect. We

learn that actions whose turpitude is very differently reputed proceed from one and the same affections. Sleep takes off the costume of circumstance, arms us with terrible freedom, so that every will rushes to a deed. A skillful man reads his dreams for his self-knowledge; yet not the details, but the quality. What part does he play in them—a cheerful, manly part, or a poor-driveling part? However monstrous and grotesque their apparitions, they have a substantial truth. The same remark may be extended to the omens and coincidences which may have astonished us. Of all it is true that the reason of them is always latent in the individual. Goethe said: "These whimsical pictures, inasmuch as they originate from us, may well have an analogy with our whole life and fate.[23]

Emerson's statement is significant because he recognizes more clearly than anyone had recognized before him the connection between character and dream. Our own character is reflected in dreams and particularly those aspects of it which do not appear in our manifest behavior. So is the character of others. When awake we mostly see only their behavior and actions. We recognize in our dreams the hidden forces underlying their behavior and dreams, and therefore, will often be able to predict future actions.

I conclude this brief review of the history of dream

[*]Ralph Waldo Emerson, *Lectures and Biographical Sketches,* "Demonology." The Riverside Press, Cambridge. Houghton Mifflin Company, Boston and New York. 1883 and 1904, pp. 7 and 8.

interpretation with one of the most original and interesting theories about dreams, that of Henri Bergson. Like Nietzsche, Bergson believes that various somatic stimuli give rise to the process of dreaming; but, unlike Nietzsche, he does not believe that these stimuli are to be interpreted by the dominant cravings and passions in us, but that we select from our vast and almost unlimited store of memories those which fit into these somatic stimuli and that these forgotten memories form the contents of the dream. Bergson's theory of memory comes very close to Freud's. He, too, assumes that we forget nothing and that what we remember is only a small segment of the totality of our memory. He says:

> Our memories, at any given moment, form a solid whole, a pyramid, so to speak, whose point is inserted precisely into our present action. But behind the memories which are concerned in our present occupation and are revealed by means of it, there are others, thousands of others, stored below the scene illuminated by consciousness. Yes, I believe indeed that all our past life is there, preserved even to the most infinitesimal details, and that we forget nothing, and that all that we have felt, perceived, thought, willed, from the first awakening of our consciousness, survives indestructibly. But the memories which are preserved in these obscure depths are there in the state of invisible phantoms. They aspire, perhaps, to the light, but they do not even try to rise to it; they know that it is impossible and that I, as a living and acting being, have some-

thing else to do than to occupy myself with them. But suppose that, at a given moment, I become *disinterested* in the present situation, in the present action—in short, in all which previously had fixed and guided my memory; suppose, in other words, that I am asleep. Then these memories, perceiving that I have taken away the obstacle, have raised the trap-door which has kept them beneath the floor of consciousness, arise from the depths; they rise, they move, they perform in the night of unconsciousness a great danse macabre. They rush together to the door which has been left ajar. They all want to get through. But they cannot; there are too many of them. From the multitudes which are called, which will be chosen? It is not hard to say. Formerly when I was awake, the memories which forced their way were those which could involve claims of relationship with the present situation, with what I saw and heard around me. Now it is more vague images which occupy my sight, more indecisive sounds which affect my ear, more indistinct touches which are distributed over the surface of my body, but there are also the more numerous sensations which arise from the deepest parts of the organism. So, then, among the phantom memories which aspire to fill themselves with color, with sonority, in short with materiality, the only ones that succeed are those which can assimilate themselves with the color-dust that we perceive, the external and internal sensations

that we catch, etc., and which, besides, respond to the affective tone of our general sen-
sibility. When this union is effected between
the memory and the sensation, we have a
dream. . . .[24]

Bergson stresses the difference between the waking
and the sleeping state:

You ask me what it is that I do when I
dream? I will tell you what you do when you
are awake. You take me, the me of dreams,
me the totality of your past, and you force me,
by making me smaller and smaller, to fit into
the little circle that you trace around your present action. That is what it is to be awake.
That is what it is to live the normal psychical
life. It is to battle. It is to will. As for
the dream, have you really any need that I
should explain it? It is the state into which
you naturally fall when you let yourself go,
when you no longer have the power to con-
centrate yourself upon a single point, when
you have ceased to will. What needs much
more to be explained is the marvelous mechanism by which at any moment your will ob-
tains instantly, and almost unconsciously, the
concentration of all that you have within you
upon one and the same point, the point that
interests you. But to explain this is the task of
normal psychology, of the psychology of wak-

[24] Henri Bergson, *Dreams*. Translated by Edwin E. Slosson. (B. W.
Huebsch, New York, 1914), pp. 33, 34, 35.

ing, for willing and waking are one and the same thing.[25]

Bergson's emphasis on the nature of the waking as against that of the sleeping state is a point of view which underlies my own theory of dreams. The difference, however, is that Bergson assumes that in sleep we are simply disinterested and that somatic stimuli are the only factors we are interested in; while I assume that we are intensely interested in our own wishes, fears and insights although not in the task of mastering reality.

Even this brief sketch of the history of dream interpretation shows that in this, as in so many other areas of the science of man, we have little reason to consider our knowledge superior to that of the great cultures of the past. There are, however, some discoveries which are not to be found in any of the older theories: Freud's principle of free association as the key to the understanding of dreams and his insight into the nature of the "dream-work," particularly into such mechanisms as condensation and displacement. Even one who has been studying dreams for many years can hardly cease to be surprised when he sees how associations, coming from many different and often remote memories and experiences, fit together and make it possible to uncover the picture of the true thoughts of the sleeper underneath the manifest dream which is often unintelligible or deceptive.

As to the contents of the old dream theories, suffice it to say in summing up that one of the two views that

[25] *Ibid.*, p. 49.

dreams are either manifestations of our animal nature
—the gate of delusion—or of our most rational powers
—the gate of truth—is held by most students of dreams.
Some of them believe, like Freud, that all dreams are of
an irrational nature; others, like Jung, that they are all
revelations of higher wisdom. But many students share
the view expressed throughout this book—that dreams
partake of both, of our irrational *and* of our rational nature, and that it is the aim of the art of dream interpretation to understand when our better self and when our
animal nature makes itself heard in the dream.

VI

The Art of

Dream Interpretation

TO UNDERSTAND THE LANGUAGE OF DREAMS IS AN ART which, like any other art, requires knowledge, talent, practice and patience. Talent, the effort to practice what one has learned, and patience cannot be acquired by reading a book. But the knowledge necessary to understand dream language can be conveyed, and to do this is the purpose of this chapter. However, since this book is written for the layman and the beginning student, this chapter will attempt to give only relatively simple dream examples as illustrations of the most significant principles for the interpretation of dreams.

From our theoretical considerations about the meaning and function of the dream, it follows that one of the most significant and often most difficult problems in the interpretation of dreams is that of recognizing whether a dream is expressive of an irrational wish and its fulfillment, of a plain fear or anxiety, or of an insight into inner or outer forces and occurrences. Is the dream to be understood as the voice of our lower or our higher self? How do we go about finding out in which key to interpret the dream?

Other questions relevant to the technique of dream interpretation are: Do we need the associations of the dreamer, as Freud postulates, or can we understand the dream without them? Furthermore, what is the relation of the dream to recent events, particularly to the dreamer's experiences on the day before he had a dream, and what is its relationship to the dreamer's total personality, the fears and wishes rooted in his character?

I should like to begin with a simple dream which illustrates the fact that no dream deals with meaningless material:

> A young woman, interested in the problems of dream interpretation, tells her husband at the breakfast table: "Tonight I had a dream which shows that there are dreams which have no meaning. The dream was simply that I saw myself serving you strawberries for breakfast." The husband laughs and says: "You only seem to forget that strawberries are the one fruit which I do not eat."

It is obvious that the dream is far from being meaningless. She offers her husband something she knows he cannot accept and is of no use or pleasure to him. Does this dream indicate that she is a frustrating personality who likes to give the very thing that is not acceptable? Does it show a deep-seated conflict in the marriage of these two people, caused by her character but quite unconscious in her? Or is her dream only the reaction to a disappointment caused by her husband the day before, and an expression of a fleeting anger she got rid of in the revenge contained in the dream? We cannot answer these questions without knowing more about the dreamer and her marriage, but we do know that the dream is not meaningless.

The following dream is more complicated though not really difficult to understand:

A lawyer, twenty-eight years of age, wakes up and remembers the following dream which he later reports to the analyst: "I saw myself riding on a white charger, reviewing a large number of soldiers. They all cheered me wildly."

The first question the analyst asks his patient is rather general: "What comes to your mind?" "Nothing," the man answers. "The dream is silly. You know that I dislike war and armies, that I certainly would not want to be a general." And in addition, "I also would not like to be the center of attention and to be stared at, cheering or no cheering, by thousands of soldiers. You know from what I told you about my professional problems how difficult it is for me even to plead a case in court with everybody looking at me."

The analyst answers: "Yes, that is all quite true; but it does not do away with the fact that this is *your* dream, the plot *you* have written and in which you assigned yourself a role. In spite of all obvious inconsistencies, the dream must have some meaning and must make some sense. Let us begin with your associations to the dream contents. Focus on the dream picture, your-

self and the white charger and the troops cheering—
and tell me what comes to your mind when you see this
picture?"

"Funny, I now see a picture which I used to like
very much when I was fourteen or fifteen. It is a picture
of Napoleon, yes indeed, on a white charger, riding in
front of his troops. It is very similar to what I saw in the
dream, except in that picture the soldiers did not cheer."

"This memory is certainly interesting. Tell me more
about your liking for that picture and your interest in
Napoleon."

"I can tell you a lot about it, but I find it embarrassing. Yes, when I was fourteen or fifteen I was rather
shy. I was not very good in athletics and kind of afraid
of tough kids. Oh, yes, now I remember an incident
from that period which I had completely forgotten. I
liked one of the tough kids very much and wanted to
become his friend. We had hardly talked with each
other, but I hoped that he would like me, too, if we
would get better acquainted. One day—and it took a
lot of courage—I approached him and asked him
whether he would not like to come to my house; that I
had a microscope and could show him a lot of interesting things. He looked at me for a moment, then he suddenly started to laugh and laugh and laugh. 'You sissy,
why don't you invite some of your sisters' little friends?'
I turned away, choking with tears. It was at that time I
read voraciously about Napoleon; I collected pictures of
him and indulged in daydreams of becoming like him,
a famous general, admired by the whole world. Was he
not small of stature, too? Was he not also a shy young-

ster like myself? Why could I not become like him? I spent many hours daydreaming; hardly ever concretely about the means to this end but always about the achievement. I *was* Napoleon, admired, envied, and yet magnanimous and ready to forgive my detractors. When I went to college I had got over my hero worship and my Napoleon daydreams; in fact I have not thought of this period for many years and certainly have never spoken to anyone about it. It kind of embarrasses me even now to talk to you about it."

" 'You' forgot about it, but the other you, that which determines many of your actions and feelings, well hidden from your daytime awareness, is still longing to be famous, admired, to have power. That other you spoke up in your dream last night; but let us see why just last night. Tell me what happened yesterday that was of importance to you."

"Nothing at all; it was a day like any other. I went to the office, worked to gather legal material for a brief, went home and had dinner, went to a movie and went to bed. That's all."

"That does not seem to explain why you rode on a white charger in the night. Tell me more about what went on at the office."

"Oh, I just remember . . . but this can't have anything to do with the dream . . . well, I'll tell you anyway. When I went to see my boss—the senior partner of the firm—for whom I collected the legal material, he discovered a mistake I had made. He looked at me critically and remarked, 'I am really surprised—I had thought you would do better than that.' For the moment

I was quite shocked—and the thought flashed through my mind that he would not take me into the firm as a partner later on as I had hoped he would do. But I told myself that this was nonsense, that anyone could make a mistake, that he had just been irritable and that the episode had no bearing on my future. I forgot about the incident during the afternoon."

How was your mood then? Were you nervous or kind of depressed?"

"No, not at all. On the contrary, I was just tired and sleepy. I found it difficult to work and was very glad when the time came to leave the office."

"The last thing of importance during that day, then, was your seeing the movie. Will you tell me what it was?"

"Yes, it was the film *Juarez*, which I enjoyed very much. In fact, I cried quite a bit."

"At what point?"

"First at the description of Juarez's poverty and suffering and then when he had been victorious; I hardly remember a movie which moved me so much."

"Then you went to bed, fell asleep, and saw yourself on the white charger, cheered by the troops. We understand a little better now why you had this dream, don't we? As a boy you felt shy, awkward, rejected. We know from our previous work that this had a great deal to do with your father, who was so proud of his success but so incapable of being close to you and of feeling— to say nothing of showing—affection and of giving encouragement. The incident you mentioned today, the rejection by the tough kid, was only the last straw, as it

were. Your self-esteem had been badly damaged already, and this episode added one more element to
make you certain that you could never be your father's
equal, never amount to anything, that you would always be rejected by the people you admired. What
could you do? You escaped into fantasy where you
achieved the very things you felt incapable of achieving
in real life. There, in the world of fantasy where nobody
could enter and where nobody could disprove you, you
were Napoleon, the great hero, admired by thousands
and—what is perhaps the most important thing—by
yourself. As long as you could retain these fantasies
you were protected from the acute pains that your feeling of inferiority caused you while you were in contact
with the reality outside yourself. Then you went to college. You were less dependent on your father, felt some
satisfaction in your studies, felt that you could make a
new and better beginning. Moreover, you felt ashamed
of your 'childish' daydreams, so you put them away;
you felt you were on the way to being a real man. . . .
But, as we have seen, this new confidence was somewhat deceptive. You were terribly frightened before
every examination; you felt that no girl could really be
interested in you if there was any other young man
around; you were always afraid of your boss's criticism.
This brings us to the day of the dream. The thing you
tried so hard to avoid had happened—your boss had
criticized you; you began to feel again the old feeling of
inadequacy, but you shoved it away; you felt tired instead of feeling anxious and sad. Then you saw a movie
which touched upon your old daydreams, the hero who

became the admired savior of a nation after he had been the despised, powerless youngster. You pictured yourself, as you had done in your adolescence, as the hero, admired, cheered. Don't you see that you have not really given up the old retreat into fantasies of glory; that you have not burned the bridges that lead you back to that land of fantasy, but start to go back there whenever reality is disappointing and threatening? Don't we see that this fact, however, helps to create the very danger you are so afraid of, that of being childish, not an adult, not being taken seriously by grown-up men—and by yourself?"

This dream is very simple, and for this reason permits us to study the various elements that are significant in the art of dream interpretation. Is this a dream of wish-fulfillment or is it an insight? The answer can hardly be in doubt: this is the fulfillment of an irrational wish for fame and recognition which the dreamer had developed as a reaction to severe blows to his self-confidence. The irrational nature of this wish is indicated by the fact that he does not choose a symbol which in reality could be meaningful and attainable. He is not really interested in military matters, has not made and certainly will not make the slightest effort to become a general. The material is taken from the immature daydreaming of an insecure, adolescent boy.

What role do his associations play in the understanding of this dream? Could we understand it even if we had no associations from the dreamer? The symbols used in the dream are universal symbols. The man on the white charger, cheered by troops, is a universally understood symbol of splendor, power, admiration (universally, of course, in the restricted sense of being common to some cultures but not necessarily to all). From his associations about his Napoleon worship, we gain further insight into the choice of this specific symbol and into its psychological function. If we did not have this association, we could only say that the dreamer had a fantasy of fame and power. In connection with his adolescent Napoleon worship, we understand that this dream symbolism is the revival of an old fantasy which had the function of compensating for a feeling of defeat and powerlessness.

We recognize also the significance of the connection of the dream and significant experiences during the preceding day. Consciously the dreamer pushed out of his mind the feeling of disappointment and apprehension at his boss's criticism. The dream shows us that the criticism had hit him again at his sensitive spot, the fear of inadequacy and failure, and had reproduced the old avenue of escape, the daydream of fame. This daydream was always latently present, but it became manifest only—and thus appeared in a dream—because of an experience which actually occurred in reality. There is hardly any dream which is not a reaction—often a delayed reaction—to a significant experience of the preceding day. In fact, often only the dream shows that an occurrence, which consciously was not experienced as being significant, actually was important, and indicates what its importance consisted of. A dream, in order to be fully understood, must be understood in terms of the reaction to a significant event which happened before the dream occurred.

We find here still another connection—though of a different kind—with an experience of the preceding day: the movie that contained material similar to that of the dreamer's daydreams. It is startling again and again to see how the dream succeeds in weaving different threads into one fabric. Would the dreamer not have had this dream had he not seen the movie? It is impossible to answer this question. Undoubtedly, the experience with his boss and the deeply engraved grandiose fantasy could have been sufficient to produce this dream; but perhaps the movie was necessary to revive the grandiose fantasy so articulately. But it is not important to answer the question, even if it could be answered. What is important is to understand the texture of the dream in which past and present, character and realistic event, are woven together into a design which tells us a great deal about the motivation of the dreamer, the dangers he must be aware of, and the aims he must set himself in his effort to achieve happiness.

The following dream is another illustration of dreams to be understood in Freud's sense of wish-fulfillment. The dreamer, a man, thirty years old, unmarried, suffered for many years from severe attacks of anxiety, an overwhelming sense of guilt, and almost continuous suicidal fantasies. He felt guilty because of what he called his badness, his evil strivings; accused himself of wanting to destroy everything and everybody, of the wish to kill children, and in his fantasies

suicide seemed the only way to protect the world from
his evil presence and to atone for his badness. There
is another aspect of these fantasies, though: after his
sacrificial death he would be reborn into an all-power-
ful, all-loved person, vastly superior in power, wisdom
and goodness to all other men. The dream he had at an
early period of analytic work was as follows:

> I am walking up a mountain; right and
> left beside the road are the bodies of dead
> men. None is alive. When I arrive at the top
> of the mountain, I find my mother sitting
> there; I am suddenly a very small child and
> am sitting on my mother's lap.

The dreamer woke from his dream with a feeling
of fright. At the time of his dream, he was so tortured
by anxiety that he could not associate with a single part
of the dream nor discover any specific event of the preceding day. But the meaning of the dream is transparent if we consider the thoughts and fantasies the
dreamer presented before the time of this dream. He
is the older son, a younger brother having been born a
year after him. The father, an authoritarian, strict minister, had little love for the older boy—or for anyone
else, for that matter; his only contact with his son was
to teach, scold, admonish, ridicule and punish. The
child was so afraid of him that he believed his mother
when she told him that had it not been for her inter-
vention his father would have killed him. The mother
was very different from the father: a pathologically pos-
sessive woman, disappointed in her marriage, with no

interest in anyone or anything except the possession of her children. But she had fastened herself particularly on this first-born son. She frightened him by telling about dangerous ghosts, then offered herself as his protectress who would pray for him, guide him, make him strong, so that one day he would even be stronger than his dreaded father. When the little brother was born, the boy was apparently profoundly disturbed and jealous. He himself had no memories of that period, but relatives reported unmistakable expressions of intense jealousy shortly after the brother's birth.

This jealousy might not have developed to such dangerous dimensions as it did after two or three years had it not been for the attitude of his father who picked the newborn baby as *his*. Why, we do not know; perhaps because of the striking physical likeness to himself or perhaps because his wife was still so preoccupied with *her* favorite son. By the time our dreamer was four or five years old, the rivalry between the two brothers was already in full swing and it increased from year to year. The antagonism between the parents was reflected and fought out in the antagonism between the two brothers. At that age the foundations of the dreamer's later severe neurosis were laid: intense hostility against the brother, a passionate wish to prove that he was superior to the brother, intense fear of the father, greatly increased by the guilt feeling because of his hate against brother and the hidden wish to be stronger than the father eventually. This feeling of anxiety, guilt and powerlessness was increased by his mother. As already mentioned, she instilled him with even more fear. But she offered him also an alluring solution: if he remained her baby, possessed by her and with no other interest, she would make him great, superior to the hated rival. This was the basis for his daydreams of greatness as well as for the tie that kept him closely bound to his mother—a state of childish dependency and a refusal to accept his role as a grown-up man.

Against this background the dream is easily understandable. "He climbs up the hill"—his ambition to be superior to everybody, the goal of his strivings. "There are many male bodies—every one is dead—none is alive." The fulfillment of his wish for elimination of all rivals—since he feels so powerless he can be safe from them only if they are dead. "When he arrives at the top"—when he achieves the goal of his wishes—"he finds his mother there, and he is sitting on her lap"—he is reunited with his mother, her baby, getting her strength and protection. All rivals are done away with—he is alone with her, free, without reason for fear. Yet he wakes with a feeling of terror. The very fulfillment of his irrational wishes is a threat to his rational, grown-up personality, which is striving for health and happiness. The price of the fulfillment of infantile desires is that he remain the baby, helplessly tied to and dependent on his mother, not permitted to think for himself or to love anyone else. The very fulfillment of his wishes is terrifying.

The difference between this dream and the previous one is considerable in one respect. The first dreamer is a shy, inhibited person, experiencing difficulties in living which spoil his happiness and weaken him. An insignificant incident like his boss's criticism hurts him deeply and throws him back to early day-dreams. On the whole, he functions normally and such an incident is needed to bring his grandiose fantasies back to his awareness in his sleep life. Our second dreamer is sicker. His whole life, in sleep and in waking, is obsessed by fear, guilt, and an intense long-ing to return to his mother. No particular incident is needed to produce the dream; almost any occurrence can serve because he experiences his life not in terms of reality but in the light of his early experiences.

In other respects the two dreams are similar. They represent the fulfillment of irrational desires, dating back to childhood, the first arousing satisfaction because of the wish's compatibility with adult conventional aims (power, prestige), the second arousing anxiety because of its very incompatibility with any kind of adult life. Both dreams speak in universal symbols and can be understood without associations, although, in order to understand fully the significance of each dream, we need to know something about the dreamer's personal history. But then, even if we knew nothing about the dreamers' histories, we would get some idea about their characters from these dreams.

Here are two brief dreams, the text of which is sim-ilar and yet the meaning of each is different from that of the other. Both are dreams of a young homosexual The first dream:

I see myself with a pistol in my hand.
The barrel is strangely elongated.

The second dream:

> I hold a long and heavy stick in my hand.
> It feels as if I were beating someone—although there is nobody else in the dream.

If we followed Freud's theory, we would assume that both dreams express a homosexual wish, one time the pistol and the other time the stick symbolizing the male genital. When the patient was asked what came to his mind of the events of the preceding days, respectively, he reported two very different occurrences:

In the evening preceding the pistol dream he had seen another young man and had felt an intense sexual urge. Before falling asleep he had indulged in sexual fantasies with this young man as the object.

The discussion of the second dream, approximately two months later, elicited a rather different association. He had been furious with his college professor because he felt he had been treated unfairly. He was too timid to say anything to the professor but had an elaborate daydream of revenge in the period before falling asleep, which period was frequently devoted to daydreaming. Another association that came up in connection with the stick was the memory that a teacher whom he disliked thoroughly when he was ten had once whipped another boy with a stick. He had always been afraid of that teacher, and this very fear had prevented him from giving expression to his rage.

What does the symbol of the stick mean in the second dream? Is the stick also a sexual symbol? Does this dream express a well-hidden homosexual desire, the object of which is the college professor and perhaps, in his childhood, the hated teacher? If we assume that the events of the preceding day and especially the mood of the dreamer just before falling asleep are important clues for the symbolism of the dream, then we shall translate the symbols differently in spite of their apparent similarity.

The first dream followed a day in which the dreamer had homosexual fantasies, and the pistol with the elongated barrel must be assumed to symbolize a penis. It is not accidental, though, that the sexual organ is represented by a weapon. This symbolic equation indicates something important about the psychic forces underlying the dreamer's homosexual cravings. To him sexuality is an expression not of love but of a wish for domination and destruction. The dreamer, for reasons we need not discuss here, had always feared not being adequate as a male. Early guilt feelings because of masturbation, fears that he was thus harming his sexual organs, later fear that his penis was inferior in size to that of other boys, intense jealousy of men—all had combined in a wish for intimacy with men in which he could show his superiority and use his sexual organ as a powerful weapon.

The second dream had a quite different emotional background. There he was angry when falling asleep; he had been inhibited in expressing his anger; he was even inhibited in expressing his anger directly in his sleep by dreaming that he was beating the professor with the stick; he dreamed that he held the stick and had the feeling of beating "someone." The particular choice of the stick as a symbol of anger was determined by the earlier experience with the hated teacher who beat the other boy; the present anger at the professor became blended with the past anger at the school-teacher. The two dreams are interesting because they exemplify the general principle that similar symbols can have different meanings, and that the right interpretation depends on the state of mind that was predominant before the dreamer fell asleep and hence continued to exercise its influence during sleep.

Here follows a short dream which also represents a fulfillment of an irrational wish and is in extreme contrast to the feelings the dreamer is aware of:

The dreamer is an intelligent young man who came for analytic treatment because of a rather vague feeling of depression, although he functions "normally"—if the word "normal" is used in a superficial, conventional sense. He finished his studies two years before he began the analysis, and since then has worked in a position which corresponds with his interests and is favorable as far as conditions of work, salary, etc., are concerned. He is considered a good, even a brilliant worker. But this external picture is deceptive. He has a constant feeling of uneasiness, feels that he does not do as well as he could (which is true), feels depressed in spite of his apparent success. Particularly troublesome to him is his relationship to his boss, who tends to be somewhat authoritarian although within reasonable limits. The patient oscillates between attitudes of rebelliousness and submission. He often feels that unfair demands are made upon him even when this is not the case; he then tends to sulk or become argumentative; sometimes he makes mistakes unwittingly in the performance of such "forced labor." On the other hand, he is overpolite, close to being submissive to his boss and other persons in authority; quite in contrast to his rebellious attitude, he overadmires his chief and is inordinately happy when praised by him. The constant alternation between these two attitudes causes quite a strain and aggravates the depressed mood. It must be added that the patient, who came from Germany after Hitler's rise, was an ardent anti-Nazi; not just in the conventional sense of an anti-Nazi "opinion" but passionately and intelligently. This political conviction was perhaps freer from doubt than anything else he thought and felt. One can imagine the surprise and shock when one morning he remembered clearly and vividly this dream:

> I sat with Hitler, and we had a pleasant and interesting conversation. I found him charming and was very proud that he listened with great attention to what I had to say.

When questioned as to what he did say to Hitler, he replied that he had not the faintest memory of the content of the conversation. Unquestionably this dream is the fulfillment of a wish. What is remarkable about it is that his wish is so utterly alien to his conscious thinking, and that it is presented in the dream in such undisguised form.

Surprising as this dream was for the dreamer at the moment, it is not quite so puzzling to us if we consider the total character structure of the dreamer, even though only based on the few data communicated here. His central problem is that of his attitude toward authority: he exhibits an alternation of rebelliousness and submissive admiration in his daily experience. Hitler stands for the extreme form of irrational authority, and the dream shows us clearly that, in spite of the dreamer's hate against him, the submissive side is real and strong. The dream offers us a more adequate appreciation of the strength of submissive tendencies than the evaluation of the conscious material permits.

Does this dream mean that the dreamer is "really" pro-Nazi and that his hate against Hitler is "only" a conscious cover for his underlying feelings, which are the true ones? I raise this question because the dream permits us to discuss a problem of great significance for the interpretation of all dreams.

Freud's answer to this question could be very illuminating. He would say that it is not really Hitler the patient is dreaming about. Hitler is a symbol for someone else; he stands for the young man's hated and admired father. In the dream the patient uses, as it were, the convenient Hitler symbol to express feelings which belong not to the present but to the past, not to his existence as a grown-up person but to the incapsulated child in him. Freud would add that this is not different from the patients feelings toward his chief; they too, have nothing to do with the chief but are transferred from the patient's father.

In a sense all this is quite true. The blend of rebelliousness and submissiveness came into existence and developed in the relationship to the patient's father. But the old attitude still exists and is felt in reference to people with whom the patient comes in contact. *He* is still prone to rebel and to submit; he and not a child in him or "the unconscious" or whatever name we give to a person allegedly *in* him but not *him*. The past is significant—aside from a historical interest—only inasmuch as it is still present, and this is the case with the authority complex of our dreamer.

If we cannot simply say that it is not he but the child in him that wants to be on friendly terms with Hitler, does the dream not become a powerful witness against the dreamer? Does it not tell us that, in spite of all his protestations to the contrary, the dreamer "deep down" is a Nazi and only "superficially" believes himself to be Hitler's enemy?

Such a view does not take into account an important factor in the interpretation of dreams, the *quantitative element*. Dreams are like a microscope through which we look at the hidden occurrences in our soul. A comparatively small trend in the complex texture of desires and fears may be shown in the dream as having the same magnitude as another one which is of much greater weight in the dreamer's psychic system. A comparatively small annoyance with another person, for instance, may give rise to a dream in which the other person falls sick and thus is incapable of annoying us, and yet this would not mean that we have such a strong anger against that person that we "really" want him to be sick. Dreams give us a clue to the qualities of hidden desires and fears but not to their quantities; they permit of qualitative but not of quantitative analysis. In order to determine the quantity of a trend discovered qualitatively in a dream, other aspects must be taken into account: repetition of this or similar themes in other dreams, associations of the dreamer, his behavior in real life, or whatever else—like resistance to the analysis of such a trend—may help to get a better view of the intensity of desires and fears. Moreover, it is not even enough to consider the intensity of a desire; in order to judge its role and function in the whole psychic fabric, we must know those forces which have been built against this trend, combatting it and defeating it as a motive for action. Even this is not enough. We must know whether these defense forces operating against irrational desires are mainly rooted in fear of punishment and loss of love, and to what extent they are based on the presence of constructive forces opposing the irrational, repressed forces; speaking more specifically, whether instinctive trends are curbed and repressed by fear and/or by the presence of stronger forces of love and tenderness. All such considerations are imperative if we are to go beyond the qualitative analysis of dreams to the quantitative inquiry into the weight of any irrational desire.

To return to the man who dreamed about Hitler. His dream does not prove that his anti-Nazi feelings were not true, or that they were not strong. But it does show that the dreamer was still coping with a desire to submit to irrational authority, even to one he hated intensely, wishing that he might find this authority not as obnoxious as he thought.

Thus far I have presented only dreams to which Freud's wish-fulfillment theory applies. They were all the hallucinatory fulfillment of irrational wishes, during sleep. They were understood with a great deal less associative material than Freud usually presents: this was done because in two dreams quoted earlier—that of the "Botanical Monograph" and the "Uncle" dream—we have seen illustrations of dreams in which associations play an indispensable role. Now I shall proceed to discuss some dreams which also are the fulfillment of wishes, but in which the wishes do not have the irrational character they had in the dreams quoted so far.

A striking illustration of this kind of wish-fulfilling dream is the following:

> I am witnessing an experiment. A man has been changed into stone. Then a sculptress has chiseled the stone into a figure. Suddenly the sculpture becomes alive and walks toward the sculptress in great rage. I am looking on with horror and see how he kills the sculptress. He then turns against me, and I think if I succeed in getting him into the living room where my parents are, I'll be saved. I wrestle with him and do succeed in getting him into the living room. My parents sit there with a few of their friends. But they hardly look up when they see me fighting for my life. I think: Well, I could have known long ago that they do not care. I smile triumphantly.

Here the dream ends. We must know something about the person of the dreamer to understand the dream. He is a young doctor of twenty-four, living a routine existence, completely under the domination of his mother, who runs the whole family. He does not think or feel spontaneously, goes to the hospital dutifully, is well liked because of his unassuming behavior, but he feels tired, depressed, and sees not much point in living. He is the obedient son, who stays at home, does what mother expects and has hardly any life of his own. His mother encourages him to go out with girls, but she finds fault with each one in whom he shows a little interest. Once in a while, when mother is more demanding than usual, he gets angry at her; she shows him how much he has hurt her, how ungrateful he is, and thus such outbursts of anger result in an orgy of remorse and intensified submission to her. The day before he had this dream, he had waited for a subway train. He watched three men about his age chatting on the platform. They were obviously clerks coming home from the store. They talked about the boss; one spoke of his chances for a salary raise because the boss liked him so much, another about the fact that the other day the boss had talked with him about politics. The whole conversation was that of routinized, empty little men whose life was absorbed by the triviality of the store and its boss. Our dreamer watching these men suddenly was shocked. It occurred to him: "That's me; that's my life! I am not any better than these three clerks; I am just as dead!" The dream occurred the following night.

Knowing the general psychic situation of the dreamer and the immediate precipitating cause of the dream, it is not difficult to understand the dream. He realizes that he has been turned into stone; he does not feel anything nor have any thought that is his own. He feels dead. He then recognizes that a woman is chiseling the stone into a sculpture. Quite obviously this symbol refers to his mother and what she has done to him. He recognizes the extent to which she has made him into a lifeless figure, but one which she could possess entirely. While in waking life he had sometimes complained about her demands, he had not been aware of the extent to which he had been molded by her. So far the dream contains an insight far truer and clearer than what he knew in waking life: an insight about his own situation and the role of his mother in his life. Then the situation changes. The dreamer appears in two roles (as often happens in dreams). He is the onlooker who observes what goes on, but he is also the statue that has come to life and in violent rage killed the sculptress. Here he experiences a rage against his mother which had been completely repressed. Neither he nor anyone else would have thought him capable of such rage, or that his mother could be the target. In the dream he experiences his rage not as his own but as that of the statue brought to life. "He," the onlooker, is terrified of the enraged man who then turns against him.

This splitting of one person into two, which occurs so plainly in the dream, is an experience all of us have more or less distinctly. The dreamer is afraid of his own rage; in fact this rage is so alien to his conscious thinking that he experiences the enraged man as a different person. Yet the enraged man is "he," the forgotten, furious "he," who comes to life in the dream. The dreamer, the observer, the man he is in his daily life, feels threatened by this rage and is afraid—afraid of himself. He wrestles with himself and he hopes that by bringing the conflict, the "enemy," to his parents, he will be saved. This idea is expressive of the wishes that govern his life.

If you have to make a decision, if you cannot cope with difficulties, run to your parents, run to any authority; they will tell you what to do, they will save you—even though the price is continuous dependence and unhappiness. In deciding to get the attacker into the living room he follows an old, always-used device. But once he sees his parents, he has an entirely new and startling insight: his parents—and particularly his mother, from whom he had expected help, protection, advice, on whose wisdom and love everything seemed to depend—these same parents don't even look up; they do not care and cannot help. He is alone and must take care of his life by himself; all his hopes in the past were an illusion, which is now suddenly shattered. But this very insight, which is in a sense bitter and disappointing, makes him feel as if he had won; he smiles triumphantly because he has seen something of the truth and taken a first step into freedom.

This dream contains a mixture of motivations. There are profound insights into himself and his parents which go beyond anything he has known so far. He sees his own frozenness and deadness, sees the way his mother has molded him according to her own wishes, and he recognizes finally how little they care and how little they are able to help. So far the dream is one of those dreams whose contents are not wish-fulfillment but insight. But there is also an element of wish-fulfillment. His rage, repressed in waking life, comes to the fore, and he sees himself as overpowering and killing his mother. The wish for revenge is fulfilled in the dream.

This analysis of the wish does not seem to be different from previous illustrations of the fulfillment of irrational desires in a dream. But in spite of the apparent similarity, there is a significant difference. If we recall the dream of the white charger, for instance, the wish fulfilled was the childish grandiosity of the dreamer. Its wish does not lie in the direction of growth and self-fulfillment but is only the satisfaction of his irrational self, which recoils from the tests of reality. Or the man who dreamed of his friendly talk with Hitler only satisfied his most irrational wish, that of submission even to a hated authority.

The rage against the sculptress, experienced in the dream we are now discussing, is of a different kind. The dreamer's rage against his mother is, in a sense, irrational. It is the result of his own inability to be independent, of his capitulation before her and the ensuing unhappiness. But there is another aspect to it. His mother is a domineering woman whose influence on this boy started at a time when he could not have withstood her very well. Here, as always in the relation between children and parents, the parents are the stronger ones as long as the child is little. By the time he is old enough to give expression to his own will, so much damage has been done to that will and self-assertion that he cannot "will" any more. Once the constellation of submission-domination is established, rage necessarily follows. If the rage were permitted to be felt consciously, it could be the basis for a healthy rebellion; it would lead to a reorientation in terms of asserting himself and eventually of reaching freedom and maturity. Once this aim is reached, the rage will disappear and make place for an understanding, if not friendly, attitude toward the mother. Thus, while this rage is in itself a symptom of lacking self-assertion, it is a necessary step in the healthy development and is not irrational. In the case of this dreamer, however, the rage was repressed; fear of mother and dependence on her guidance and authority made the dreamer unaware of it, and the rage lived a secret existence far below the surface where the dreamer could never reach it. In his dream, moved by the frightening and enlightening vision of his own deadness, he and his rage both come to life. This rage is a necessary transitory stage in his process of growth and therefore fundamentally different from those desires dealt with in the previous dreams, the fulfillment of which leads backward, not forward.

The dreamer of the following dream is a man who was suffering from an intense feeling of guilt; he still, at the age of forty, reproached himself as having been responsible for his father's death twenty years before. He had gone on a trip and during his absence his father had died of a heart attack. He felt then, and still feels, that he was responsible, inasmuch as his father perhaps became excited and hence died, while if he, the son, had been there he could have averted any kind of excitement.

This dreamer is always afraid that by some fault of his another person is sick or some other damage is done. He has a vast number of private rituals whose function it is to atone for his "sins" and to avert the evil consequences of his doings. He rarely permits himself any pleasure, and enjoyment is possible only when he has managed to classify pleasure under "duty." He works excessively hard; he has only occasional and superficial sexual affairs with women, which usually end with the depressing fear that he has hurt the girl and that she now hates him. After a considerable amount of analytic work he had the following dream:

> A crime has been committed. I do not remember what the crime was, and I do not think I knew in the dream, either. I walk in the street and, although I am sure I have not committed any crime, I know that if a detective came up and accused me of murder I would not be able to defend myself. I walk faster and faster toward the river. Suddenly when I am close to the river I see in the distance a hill on which there is a beautiful city. Light radiates from the hill, I see people dancing in the streets, I feel that if I can only cross the river everything will be all right.

Analyst: "What a surprise! This is the first time you have been convinced that you did not commit a crime and that you are only afraid you could not defend yourself against the accusation. Did anything good happen yesterday?"

Patient: "Nothing of importance, except that I got

some satisfaction in establishing the fact that an oversight which had occurred in the office was definitely due to somebody else's mistake and not to mine, as I had feared they might think."

Analyst: "I can see that that is rather satisfactory —but perhaps you'll tell me what the oversight was."

Patient: "A lady phoned and wanted to see one partner of our firm, Mr. X. I spoke to her and was quite impressed by her lovely voice. I told her to come the next day at four and put a note on Mr. X's desk. Mr. X's secretary took the note, but instead of telling him, she had put the note away and entirely forgotten about it. The next day the young lady came and was hurt and distressed when she heard that Mr. X was not in and that the whole matter had been forgotten. I spoke to her and apologized and after a few minutes I induced her to tell me the problem she was going to discuss with Mr. X. All this was yesterday."

Analyst: "I take it, then, that the secretary remembered that she had neglected the matter and told you or the young lady about it?"

Patient: "Oh, yes, of course; funny that I forgot to tell this; it seemed the most important thing yesterday except—but that is nonsense."

Analyst: "Let us hear the nonsense. You know from experience that our nonsense is usually the wisest voice in us."

Patient: "Well, what I was going to say was that I felt strangely happy while I was talking to the lady. Hers was a divorce case and from what I gathered she had been coaxed and browbeaten into an impossible marriage by her ambitious mother. She had stood it for four years and now had decided to put an end to it."

Analyst: "So, you have visions of freedom, too, have you not? I am interested in a little detail. You see people dancing in the streets as the only detail of the city you recognize. Have you ever seen such a scene?"

Patient: "Wait a minute . . . that is strange . . . now I get it. . . . Yes, when I was fourteen I was with my father on a trip in France; we were in a little town on the Fourteenth of July, saw the celebration, and in the evening watched the people dance in the streets. You know, that was the last time I can remember real happiness."

Analyst: "Well, so last night you were able to pick up the thread. You could visualize freedom, light, happiness, dancing, as a possibility, as something you had experienced once and could experience again."

Patient: "Provided I know how to cross the river!"

Analyst: "Yes, that's where you stand now: for the first time you recognize that you have not really committed the crime, that there is the city in which you are free, and that a river which can be crossed separates you from this better life. No alligators in the river?"

Patient: "No, it was an ordinary river, in fact like the river in our town I was always a little afraid of as a child."

Analyst: "Then there must be a bridge. You certainly have waited a long time to cross the bridge. The problem now is to discover what still hinders you from doing so."

This is one of those important dreams in which a decisive step away from mental illness is taken. To be sure, the patient is not yet well, but he has experienced the most important thing short of being well, a clear and vivid vision of a life in which he is not the haunted criminal but a free person. He also visualizes that, in order to get there, he must cross a river, an old and universally used symbol of an important decision, of starting a new form of existence—birth or death—of giving up one form of life for another. The vision of the city is a fulfillment of a wish, but this wish is rational; it represents life; it comes from that part of the dreamer which was hidden and alienated from himself. This vision is real, as real as anything his eyes see during the day, except that he still needs the solitude and freedom of sleep existence to be sure of it.

Here is another "crossing the river" dream. The dreamer is an only, spoiled child, a boy. He was pampered by his parents, admired by them as a future genius, everything made easy, and no effort expected—from the breakfast, which his mother brought to his bed in the morning, to the father's talks with teachers, which always ended in the expression of his conviction of the boy's wonderful gifts. Both parents were morbidly afraid of danger for him; he was not permitted to swim, to hike, to play in the street. He wanted to rebel sometimes against the embarrassing restrictions, but why complain when he had all these wonderful things: admiration, affectionate caresses, so many toys that he could throw them away, and almost complete protection from all outer dangers. He actually was a gifted boy, but he had never quite succeeded in standing on his own feet. Instead of mastering things, his aim was to win applause and admiration. Thus he became dependent on others and—afraid.

But the very need for praise and the fear engendered when it was not forthcoming made him furious and even cruel. He had entered analytic treatment because of the uneasiness that was constantly produced by his childish grandiosity, dependence, fear and rage. After six months of analytic work he had the following dream.

> I am to cross a river. I look for a bridge, but there is none. I am small, perhaps five or six. I cannot swim. [He actually learned how to swim at eighteen.] Then I see a tall, dark man who makes a sign that he can carry me over in his arms. [The river is only about five feet deep.] I am glad for the moment and let him take me. While he holds me and starts walking, I am suddenly seized by panic. I know that if I don't get away I shall die. We are already in the river, but I muster all my courage and jump from the man's arms into the water. At first I think I'll be drowned. But then I start swimming, and soon reach the other shore. The man has disappeared.

The preceding day the dreamer had been at a party, and it had suddenly dawned upon him that all his interests were directed to the goal of being admired and liked. He had felt—for the first time—how childish he really was and that he had to make a decision. Yes.

he could go on being the irresponsible child, or he could accept the painful transition to maturity. He felt he must not kid himself any longer that everything was as it should be and mistake his success in pleasing for real achievement. These thoughts had quite shaken him, and he had fallen asleep.

The dream is not difficult to understand. Crossing the river is the decision he must make to cross from the shore of childhood to that of maturity. But how can he do it if he thinks himself five or six, when he could not swim. The man who offers to carry him stands for many persons: father, teachers, everyone who was ready to carry him—bribed by his charm and promise. So far the dream symbolizes accurately his inner problem and the way he has solved it again and again. But now a new factor enters. He realizes that if he permits himself to be carried again he will be destroyed. This insight is sharp and clear. He feels that he has to make a decision, and he jumps into the water. He is aware that he really can swim (apparently he is no longer five or six in the dream) and that he can reach the other shore without help. This again is wish-fulfillment but, as in the previous dream, it is a vision of his goal as an adult; it is a keen awareness of the fact that his accustomed method of being carried must lead to ruin; furthermore, he knows that he actually can swim if he only has the courage to jump.

Needless to say, as the days went by the vision lost its original clarity. The daytime "noises" suggested that one must not be "extreme," that all was going well, that there was no reason to give up all friendship, that we all need help and that he certainly deserved it, and so on—these and many other reasons which we manufacture in order to befog a clear but uncomfortable insight. After quite some time, though, he was as wise and courageous during the daytime as he had been in the night—and the dream came true.

These last dreams illustrate an important point, the difference between rational and irrational wishes. We often wish things that are rooted in our weakness and compensate for it; we dream of ourselves as famous, all powerful, loved by everybody, etc. But sometimes we dream of wishes which are the anticipation of our most valuable goals. We can see ourselves as dancing or flying; we see the city of light; we experience the happy presence of friends. Even if we are not yet capable in our waking life to experience the joy of the dream, the dream experience shows that we are at least capable of wishing it and seeing it fulfilled in a dream fantasy. Fantasies and dreams are the beginning of many deeds, and nothing would be worse than to discourage or depreciate them. What matters is the kind of fantasy which we have—does it lead us forward or does it hold us back in the chains of unproductiveness?

The following dream is expressive of a profound insight into the dreamer's problem and is a good illustration of the function of associative material. The dreamer, a thirty-five-year-old man, had suffered since adolescence from a mild but persistent depression. His father had been an easygoing but unloving man. His mother had suffered from severe depressions from the time the boy was eight or nine. He was not allowed to play with other children; if he went out of the house, his mother reproached him for hurting her feelings; only with books and his fantasies in one corner of a room was he safe from reproach. Any expression of enthusiasm was answered by his mother with a shrug of the shoulders and remarks to the effect that there was no particular reason for such happiness and excitement. The dreamer, while refuting his mother's reproaches with his mind, nevertheless felt that she was right and that her unhappiness was his fault. He also felt that he was ill equipped for life, since some of the essential conditions for successful living had been missing in his childhood. He was always embarrassed lest others find out about the emotional (rather than the material) poverty of his background. One problem that is particularly upsetting to him is that of communication with other people, particularly reaction to attacks or teasing. He is utterly at a loss vis-à-vis such behavior and feels at ease only with a few good friends. This is the dream:

> I see a man sitting in a wheel chair. He is beginning a game of chess but without much pleasure. He interrupts the game suddenly and says, "Two figures were removed from my set long ago. But I make up for it by 'Thessail.'" Then he adds, "A voice (my mother's) has been piped into me: 'Life is not worth living.'"

Part of the dream is readily understandable when we know something of the history and the problem of the dreamer. The man in the wheel chair is he. The game of chess is the game of life, particularly that aspect where one is attacked and has to counterattack or use some other strategy. He is not too willing to play this game, since he feels ill equipped for it. "Two figures were removed from my set long ago." This is the feeling he has also in his waking state: that he was deprived of things in his childhood, and that this is the reason for his helplessness in the battle of life. The two figures which had been removed? The king and the queen, his father and mother, who were not really there except in a negative function, to disappoint, to nag, to tease, to reproach. But he can nevertheless manage to play with the help of "Thessail." Here we are stuck, and so was the dreamer.

Patient: "I see the word clearly before me. But I haven't the slightest idea what it means."

Analyst: "You apparently knew in your dream what it meant; it is, after all, *your* dream and the word is your coinage. Let us try some free association. What comes to mind when you think of the word?"

Patient: "The first thing that occurs to me is Thessaly, a part of Greece. Yes, I remember that I was quite impressed as a kid with Thessaly. I don't know whether this is actually so or not, but I think of Thessaly as a part of Greece with a warm, even climate, where shepherds live peacefully and happily. I always preferred it to Sparta and Athens. Sparta I abhorred because of its militaristic spirit—Athens I didn't like because the Athenians seemed to me hypercultivated snobs. Yes, I felt drawn to the shepherds in Thessaly."

Analyst: "The word you dream of is 'Thessail' rather than Thessaly. Why did you change it?"

Patient: "Funny, what I think of now is a flail, the instrument the peasants use for threshing. But they can also use it as a weapon if they have nothing else."

Analyst: "That is very interesting. Thessail, then, is composed of Thess-aly and fl-ail. In a curious way Thessaly, or rather what it means to you, is closely related to the flail. Shepherds and peasants: the simple, idyllic life. Let us come back and see what you say in the dream. You play chess and know two figures have been removed from your set, but you can make up with 'Thessail.'"

Patient: "The thought is pretty clear to me now. In the game of life I feel handicapped because of the frustrations of my childhood. I do not quite have the weapons [the chess figures that have reference to a battle] others have, but if I could withdraw into a simple, idyllic life, I could even fight with a flail as a substitute for the weapons I lack—the chess figures."

Analyst: "But this is not the end of the dream. After you have interrupted your chess game you say: 'A voice has been piped into me: "Life is not worth living." '"

Patient: "This I understand very well. After all, I play the game of life only because I have to. But I am not really interested. The feeling I have had more or less strongly since my childhood is just what I say in the dream: Life is not worth living."

Analyst: "Indeed, that is what you always feel. But is there not some important message you send yourself in the dream?"

Patient: "You mean that I say that this theme of depression has been put into me by my mother."

Analyst: "Yes, that is what I mean. Once you recognize that the depressed judgment about life is not your own but your mother's voice still exercising its quasi-posthypnotic effect, you have taken one step in the direction of freeing yourself from this mood. That your depressed philosophy is not really yours is an important discovery you made—and it took the state of sleep to make it."

One type of dream for which we have given no illustration is the nightmare. In Freud's view, the anxiety dream is no exception to the general rule that the latent content of a dream is the fulfillment of an irrational wish. There is, of course, an obvious objection to this view, which will be raised by anyone who ever had a nightmare: If I go through the terrors of hell in a dream and wake up with an almost unbearable fright, does it make any sense to say that this is a wish-fulfillment?

This objection is not nearly so good as it seems on first glance. For one thing, we know of a pathological state in which people are driven to do the very thing that is destructive to them. The masochistic person has a wish—though an unconscious one—to incur an accident, to be sick, to be humiliated. In the masochistic perversion—where this wish is blended with sex and therefore less dangerous to the person—the masochistic wish is even conscious. Furthermore, we know that suicide can be the result of an overpowering impulse for revenge and destruction, directed against one's own person rather than against someone else. Yet the person driven to a self-destructive or other painful act may, with the other part of his personality, feel genuine and intense fright. This does not alter the fact that the fright is the outcome of his own self-destructive wishes. But a wish may create anxiety, so Freud observes, not only if it is a masochistic or self-destructive impulse. We may wish something but know that the gratification of the wish will make other people hate us and bring about punishment by society. Naturally, the fulfillment of this wish would produce anxiety.

An illustration of this kind of anxiety dream is offered by the following example:

> I have taken an apple from a tree while I am passing an orchard. A big dog comes and jumps at me, I am terribly frightened, and I wake up yelling for help.

All that is necessary for the understanding of the dream is the knowledge that the dreamer had met, the evening before the dream, a married woman to whom he felt greatly attracted. She seemed to be rather encouraging, and he had fallen asleep with fantasies of having an affair with her. We need not be concerned here whether the anxiety he felt in the dream was prompted by his conscience or by the fear of public opinion—the essential fact remains that the anxiety is the result of the gratification of his wish—to eat the stolen apple.

However, although many anxiety dreams can thus be understood as disguised wish-fulfillment, I doubt that this is the case with all or perhaps even most of them. If we assume dreaming to be any kind of mental activity under the condition of sleep, why should we not be as genuinely afraid of danger in our sleep as we are in our waking life?

But, someone may argue, is not all fear conditioned by our cravings? Would we be afraid if we had no "Thirst," as the Buddhists say; if we were not desiring things? Therefore, may it not be said that, in a general sense, every anxiety in waking and in dream life is the result of desires?

This argument is well taken, and if we were to say that there is no anxiety dream (or no anxiety in waking life) without the presence of desire, including the fundamental desire to live, I do not see that any objection could be made to this statement. But this general principle is not the one Freud meant with his interpretation. It may clarify the issue if we talk once more about the difference between the three kinds of anxiety dreams we have already discussed.

In the masochistic self-destructive nightmare, the wish is in itself painful and self-destructive. In the second type of anxiety dream, as the one with the apple, the wish is not in itself self-destructive, but it is of such a kind that its fulfillment causes anxiety in another part of the mental system. The dream is caused by the wish —which as a by-product generates anxiety. In the third type of anxiety dream, where one is afraid because of a real or imaged threat to life, freedom, etc., the dream is caused by the threat, while the wish to live, to be free, etc., is the all-present impulse that does not produce that specific dream. In other words, in the first and second categories the anxiety is caused by the presence of a wish; in the third category, by the presence of a danger (real or imagined), although not without the presence of the wish to live or any other of the permanent and universal desires. In this third category the anxiety dream is clearly not the fulfillment of the wish but the fear of its frustration.

The following is an anxiety dream not unlike many other nightmares. The dreamer reports:

> I am in a greenhouse. Suddenly I see a snake striking at me. My mother stands beside me and smiles maliciously at me. She walks away then without trying to help me. I run to the door only to find that the snake is already there—blocking my way. I wake up horrified.

The dreamer is a forty-five-year-old woman who suffers from severe anxiety. The outstanding feature in her history is the mutual hate between her and her mother. The feeling that her mother hated her was not something imagined. The mother was married to a man she never had liked; she was resentful of the first-born child, the dreamer, whose very existence, so she believed, forced her to continue her marriage. When the dreamer was three, she told her father something which made him suspect that his wife had an affair with another man. While the little girl did not know exactly what she had been observing and saying, intuitively she knew quite well, and the mother's rage at her was better founded than appeared on the surface. The older the girl became the more she tried to provoke her mother, and the more did her mother try to punish and eventually destroy her. Her life was a constant battle against attack. Had her father helped and supported her, the outcome might have been different. But he was himself afraid of his wife and never overtly supported his daughter. The result of all this and many other circumstances was that the daughter, a very gifted and proud person, withdrew more and more from people, felt defeated by her mother's "victory," and lived in the hope that "one day" she would be the victor. All this hate and insecurity caused a state of constant anxiety by which she was tortured both waking and sleeping.

The dream is one of the many expressions of it: She associates with the "greenhouse"—the greenhouse was on her parents' estate. She often went there alone, never with her mother. In the dream it is not her mother who is the danger but the snake. What does this mean? Apparently there is a wish for a mother who will protect her from danger. (In fact, she sometimes had daydreams that her mother would change and help her.) Here, again, she is in danger. But her mother smiles maliciously and walks away. In this malicious smile the mother shows her true colors. At first the attempt is made, as it were, to split the bad mother (the snake) from the good mother—who might help. When the mother looks at her maliciously and does not help, this illusion is destroyed, mother and snake are one and the same, forces threatening destruction. The dreamer then runs to the door, hoping to escape, but it is too late; the way is blocked. She is now shut in with a poisonous snake and a destructive mother.

In the dream the patient experiences the same anxiety she is haunted by in the daytime, except more intensely and in clear reference to her mother. Hers is not a realistic fear but a morbid anxiety. The mother is no longer a threat to her; in fact, no one threatens or endangers her. Nevertheless, she *is* frightened, and in the dream the fright breaks through. Is the dream the fulfillment of a wish? To some extent this is true. There is the wish to have the mother as protector and only when the mother, instead of helping, looks maliciously at her does the terror begin. It is her wish for the mother's love and protection that makes her afraid of the woman. If she did not want the mother any more, she would not be frightened of her either. But more important than these wishes for mother love and protection are others without which her fear of her mother could not have continued to exist: her wish for revenge, her desire to make her father see that his wife is evil, to take him away from her; not because she loves her father so much, nor because of the fixation to an early sexual attachment to him, but because of the deep humiliation by the early defeat and the feeling that only by her mother's destruction can her pride and self-confidence be restored. Why this early humiliation was and is so ineradicable, why the wish for revenge and triumph is so unconquerable, is another question, too complex to be discussed in this context. The dreamer has other anxiety dreams from which the one element contained in this dream—the wish that her mother should help --is completely absent. Such dreams are:

I am in a cage with a tiger. No one to help me.

Or:

I am walking on a narrow strip of land on a marsh. It is dark and I can't see my way. I am utterly lost and feel that I'll slip and drown if I take one more step.

Or:

I am the defendant in a trial; I am accused of murder, and I know that I am innocent. But I can see in the faces of the judge and the jury that they have already made up their minds that I am guilty. The interrogation is only a matter of form. I know that no matter what I say or any witnesses might say (I do not see any witnesses) the case is decided, and there is no point in trying to defend myself.

In all these dreams the essential factor is the feeling of complete helplessness leading to a paralysis of all functions and to panic. Inanimate objects, animals, people—they are merciless; no friend is in sight; no help to be expected. This feeling of complete powerlessness is rooted in the dreamer's inability to let go of her wish for revenge, to cease the battle with her mother. But it is in itself not the fulfillment of any wish. Here is the wish to live—hence the fear of being exposed to attacks without power to defend herself.

Dreams that are particularly interesting and significant are those recurrent dreams which some people report as going on for a period of years, sometimes as far back as they can recall. These dreams usually are expressive of the main theme, of the *leitmotif*, in a person's life, often the key to the understanding of his neurosis or of the most important aspect of his personality. Sometimes the dream remains unchanged, sometimes there are more or less subtle changes, which are indicative of the inner progress of the dreamer—or of a deterioration, as the case may be.

A girl of fifteen who grew up under the most inhuman and destructive conditions (father who beat her, alcoholic, violent; mother running away periodically with other men; no food, no clothing, dirt) tried to commit suicide at the age of ten, and after that five times more. She has had the following dream many times as long as she can remember:

> I am at the bottom of a pit. I try to climb up and have already reached the top, which I hold with my hands, when someone comes and stamps on my hands. I have to let go and fall back to the bottom of the pit.

The dream hardly needs any explanation; it fully expresses the tragedy of this young girl's life—what happened to her and how she feels. Were this a dream occuring once, we would be entitled to assume that it is expressive of a fear, which the dreamer feels once in a while, stimulated by specific, trying circumstances. As it is, the regular recurrence of the dream makes us assume that the dream situation is the central theme of the girl's life, that the dream expresses a conviction so deep and unalterable that we can understand why she has tried to commit suicide again and again.

A recurrent dream in which the theme remains the same but where there is, nevertheless, a considerable amount of change is one of a series which began with the dream:

> I am in prison—I cannot get out.

Later on the dream was:

> I want to cross the frontier—but I have no passport and am held back at the frontier.

Later still:

> I am in Europe—am at a port to take a boat—but there is no boat, and I don't see how I can leave.

The latest version of this dream was:

> I am in a city—in my home—I want to go out. When I open the door I find it difficult —I give it a hard push—it opens and I walk out.

The theme underlying all these dreams is the fear of being shut in, of being imprisoned, incapable of "getting out." What this fear means in the dreamer's life is of no importance for us in this context. What the series of dreams shows is that throughout the years the fear remained but became less intense—from being in prison to having difficulty in opening the door. While originally the dreamer feels incapable of escaping, in the last dream he can—with a little extra push—open the door and walk out. A considerable development has occurred in the dreamer during these years.

VII

Symbolic Language in Myth, Fairy Tale, Ritual and Novel

THE MYTH, LIKE THE DREAM, OFFERS A STORY OCCUR-
ring in space and time, a story which expresses, in symbolic language, religious and philosophical ideas, experiences of the soul in which the real significance of
the myth lies. If one fails to grasp the true meaning of
the myth, one finds oneself confronted with this alternative: either the myth is a prescientific, naïve picture of
the world and of history and at best a product of poeti-
cally beautiful imagination, or—and this is the attitude
of the orthodox believer—the manifest story of the myth
is true, and one must believe it as a correct report of
events which actually happened in "reality." While this
alternative seemed inescapable in the nineteenth and
the beginning of the twentieth centuries in Western culture, a new approach is taking place gradually. The emphasis is put on the religious and philosophical meaning
of the myth, and the manifest story is viewed as the
symbolic expression of this meaning. But even as far as
the manifest story is concerned, one has learned to understand that it is not just the product of fantastic im-

195

agination of "primitive" peoples, but contains cherished memories of the past. (The historic truth of some has been established by many findings from excavations in recent decades.) Foremost among those who have paved the way for a new understanding of the myth are J. J. Bachofen and Sigmund Freud. The former, with an unsurpassed penetration and brilliance, grasped the myth in its religious and psychological as well as its historical meaning. The latter helped the understanding of the myth by inaugurating an understanding of symbolic language on the basis of his interpretation of dreams. This was more of an indirect than a direct help to mythology, because Freud tended to see in the myth—as in the dream—only the expression of irrational, antisocial impulses rather than the wisdom of past ages expressed in a specific language, that of symbols.

1. *The Oedipus Myth*

The Oedipus myth offers the outstanding illustration of Freud's method of myth interpretation and at the same time an excellent opportunity for a different approach, one in which not sexual desires but one of the fundamental aspects of interpersonal relationships, the attitude toward authority, is held to be the central theme of the myth. It is at the same time an illustration of the distortions and changes that memories of older social forms and ideas undergo in the formation of the manifest text of the myth.[1]

[1] The following interpretation is taken from E. Fromm, "The Oedipus Complex and the Oedipus Myth," in Ruth Nanda Anshen, *The Family: Its Function and Destiny*, New York, Harper & Brothers, 1949.

Freud writes:

If the *Oedipus Rex* is capable of moving a modern reader or playgoer no less powerfully than it moved the contemporary Greeks, the only possible explanation is that the effect of the Greek tragedy does not depend upon the conflict between fate and human will, but upon the peculiar nature of the material by which this conflict is revealed. There must be a voice within us which is prepared to acknowledge the compelling power of fate in the Oedipus, while we are able to condemn the situations occurring in *Die Ahnfrau* or other tragedies of fate as arbitrary inventions. And there actually is a motive in the story of King Oedipus which explains the verdict of this inner voice. His fate moves us only because it might have been our own, because the oracle laid upon us before our birth the very curse which rested upon him. It may be that we are all destined to direct our first sexual impulses toward our mothers, and our first impulses of hatred and violence toward our fathers; our dreams convince us that we are. King Oedipus, who slew his father Laius and wedded his mother Jocasta, is nothing more or less than a wish-fulfillment—the fulfillment of the wish of our childhood. But we, more fortunate than he, in so far as we have not become psychoneurotics, have since our childhood succeeded in withdrawing our sexual impulses from our mothers, and in forgetting our jealousy of our fathers. We recoil from the person for whom this primitive wish of our childhood has been fulfilled with all the force of the repression which these wishes have undergone in our minds since childhood. As the poet brings the guilt of Oedipus to light by his investigation, he forces us to become aware of our own inner selves, in which the same impulses are still extant, even though they are suppressed. The antithesis with which the chorus departs:

> ". . . Behold, this is Oedipus
> Who unravelled the great riddle,
>   and was first in power,
> Whose fortune all the townsmen
>   praised and envied;
> See in what dread adversity he sank!"

. . . . this admonition touches us and our own pride, us who since the years of our childhood have grown so wise and so powerful in our own estimation. Like Oedipus, we live in ignorance of the desires that offend morality, the desires that nature has forced upon us and after their unveiling we may well prefer to avert our gaze from the scenes of our childhood.[2]

The concept of the Oedipus complex, which Freud has so beautifully presented, became one of the cornerstones of his psychological system. He believed that this concept was the key to an understanding of history and

[2] Sigmund Freud, "The Interpretation of Dreams," in *The Basic Writings of Sigmund Freud*, translated by Dr. A. A. Brill (New York, The Modern Library, 1938), p. 308.

of the evolution of religion and morality. His conviction was that this very complex constituted the fundamental mechanism in the development of the child, and he maintained that the Oedipus complex was the cause of psychopathological development and the "kernel of neurosis."

Freud referred to the Oedipus myth in the version of Sophocles's tragedy *King Oedipus*. This tragedy tells us that an oracle has told Laius, the King of Thebes, and his wife, Jocasta, that if they have a son this son will kill his father and marry his own mother. When a son, Oedipus, is born to them, Jocasta decides to escape the fate predicted by the oracle by killing the infant. She gives Oedipus to a shepherd, who is to abandon the child in the woods with his feet bound so that he will die. But the shepherd, taking pity on the child, gives the infant to a man in the service of the King of Corinth, who in turn brings him to his master. The king adopts the boy, and the young prince grows up in Corinth not knowing that he is not the true son of the King of Corinth. He is told by the oracle in Delphi that it is his fate to kill his father and to marry his mother. He decides to avoid this fate by never going back to his alleged parents. On his way back from Delphi he engages in a violent argument with an old man riding in a carriage, loses his temper, and slays the man and his servant without knowing that he has slain his father, the King of Thebes.

His wanderings lead him to Thebes. There the Sphinx is devouring the young men and women of the city, and she will cease doing so only if someone will find the right answer to a riddle she asks. The riddle is this: "What is it which first goes on four, then on two, and eventually on three?" The city of Thebes has promised that anyone who can solve the riddle and thus free the city from the Sphinx will be made king and will be given the king's widow for a wife. Oedipus undertakes the venture. He finds the answer to the riddle—which is *man*, who as a child walks on all four, as an adult on two, and in his old age on three (with a cane). The Sphinx throws herself into the ocean, the city is saved from calamity, and Oedipus becomes king and marries Jocasta, his mother.

After Oedipus has reigned happily for some time, the city is ravaged by a plague which kills many of its citizens. The seer, Theiresias, reveals that the plague is the punishment for the twofold crime which Oedipus has committed, patricide and incest. Oedipus, after having tried desperately not to see this truth, blinds himself when he is compelled to see it, and Jocasta commits suicide. The tragedy ends at the point where Oedipus has suffered punishment for a crime which he committed unknowingly and in spite of his conscious effort to avoid committing it.

Was Freud justified in concluding that this myth confirms his view that unconscious incestuous drives and the resulting hate against the father-rival are to be found in any male child? Indeed, it does seem as if the myth confirmed Freud's theory that the Oedipus complex justifiably bears its name.

If we examine the myth more closely, however, questions arise which cast some doubts on the correctness of this view. The most pertinent question is this: If Freud's interpretation is right, we should expect the myth to tell us that Oedipus met Jocasta without knowing that she was his mother, fell in love with her, and then killed his father, again unknowingly. But there is no indication whatsoever in the myth that Oedipus is attracted by or falls in love with Jocasta. The only reason we are given for Oedipus's marriage to Jocasta is that she, as it were, goes with the throne. Should we believe that a myth, the central theme of which constitutes an incestuous relationship between mother and son, would entirely omit the element of attraction between the two? This question is all the more weighty in view of the fact that, in the older versions of the oracle, the prediction of the marriage to the mother is mentioned only once in the version by Nikolaus of Damascus, which according to Carl Robert goes back to a relatively new source.[3]

Furthermore, Oedipus is described as the courageous and wise hero who becomes the benefactor of Thebes. How can we understand that the same Oedipus is described as having committed the crime most horrible in the eyes of his contemporaries? This question has sometimes been answered by pointing to the fact that the very essence of the Greek concept of tragedy is that the powerful and strong are suddenly struck by disaster. Whether such an answer is sufficient or whether another view can give us a more satisfactory answer remains to be seen.

[3] Cf. Carl Robert, *Oedipus* (Berlin: Weidmannsche Buchhandlung), 1915.

The foregoing questions arise from a consideration of *King Oedipus*. If we examine only this tragedy, without taking into account the two other parts of the trilogy, *Oedipus at Colonus* and *Antigone*, no definite answer can be given. But we are at least in a position to formulate a hypothesis, namely, *that the myth can be understood as a symbol not of the incestuous love between mother and son but of the rebellion of the son against the authority of the father in the patriarchal family; that the marriage of Oedipus and Jocasta is only a secondary element, only one of the symbols of the victory of the son, who takes his father's place and with it all his privileges.*

The validity of this hypothesis can be tested by examining the whole Oedipus myth, particularly in the form presented by Sophocles in the two other parts of his trilogy, *Oedipus at Colonus* and *Antigone*.[4]

In *Oedipus at Colonus* we find Oedipus near Athens at the grove of the Eumenides shortly before he dies. After having blinded himself, Oedipus had remained in Thebes, which was ruled by Creon, his uncle, who after some time exiled him. Oedipus's two daughters, Antigone and Ismene, accompanied him into exile; but his two sons, Eteocles and Polyneices, refused to help their blind father. After his departure, the two brothers strove for possession of the throne. Eteocles won; but Polyneices, refusing to yield, sought to con-

[4] While it is true that the trilogy was not written in this order and while some scholars may be right in their assumption that Sophocles did not plan the three tragedies as a trilogy, the three must nevertheless be interpreted as a whole. It makes little sense to assume that Sophocles described the fate of Oedipus and his children in three tragedies without having in mind an inner coherence of the whole.

quer the city with outside help and to wrest the power from his brother. In *Oedipus at Colonus* we see him approach his father, begging his forgiveness and asking his assistance. But Oedipus is relentless in his hate against his sons. In spite of the passionate pleading of Polyneices, supported by Antigone's plea, he refuses forgiveness. His last words to his son are:

> And thou—begone, abhorred of me, and unfathered!—begone, thou vilest of the vile, and with thee take these my curses which I call down on thee—never to vanquish the land of thy race, no, nor ever return to hill-girt Argos, but by a kindred hand to die, and slay him by whom thou hast been driven out. Such is my prayer; and I call the paternal darkness of dread Tartarus to take thee unto another home,—I call the spirits of this place,—I call the Destroying God, who hath set that dreadful hatred in you twain. Go, with these words in thine ears—go, and publish it to the Cadmeans all, yea, and to thine own staunch allies, that Oedipus hath divided such honours to his sons.[5]

In *Antigone* we find another father-son conflict as one of the central themes of the tragedy. Here Creon, the representative of the authoritarian principle in state and family, is opposed by his son, Haemon, who reproaches him for his ruthless despotism and his cruelty

[5] "Oedipus at Colonus," in *The Complete Greek Drama*, edited by Whitney J. Oates and Eugene O'Neill, Jr. (New York, Random House), Vol. I.

against Antigone. Haemon tries to kill his father and, failing to do so, kills himself.

We find that the theme running through the three tragedies is the conflict between father and son. In *King Oedipus*, Oedipus kills his father Laius, who had intended to take the infant's life. In *Oedipus at Colonus*, Oedipus gives vent to his intense hate against his sons, and in *Antigone* we find the same hate again between Creon and Haemon. The problem of incest exists neither in the relationship between Oedipus's sons to their mother nor in the relationship between Haemon and his mother, Eurydice. If we interpret *King Oedipus* in the light of the whole trilogy, the assumption seems plausible that the real issue in *King Oedipus*, too, is the conflict between father and son and not the problem of incest.

Freud had interpreted the antagonism between Oedipus and his father as the unconscious rivalry caused by Oedipus's incestuous strivings. If we do not accept this explanation, the problem arises as how otherwise to explain the conflict between father and son which we find in all the three tragedies. One clue is given in *Antigone*. The rebellion of Haemon against Creon is rooted in the particular structure of Creon's relationship to Haemon. Creon represents the strictly authoritarian principle both in the family and in the state, and it is against this type of authority that Haemon rebels. An analysis of the whole Oedipus trilogy will show that the struggle against paternal authority is its main theme and that the roots of this struggle go far back into the ancient fight between the patriarchal and matriarchal systems of society. Oedipus, as well as Haemon and Antigone, is representative of the matriarchal principle; they all attack a social and religious order based on the powers and privileges of the father, represented by Laius and Creon.

Since this interpretation is based on Bachofen's analysis of Greek mythology, it is necessary to acquaint the reader briefly with the principles of Bachofen's theory.

In his *Mutterrecht* (Mother Right), published in 1861, Bachofen suggested that in the beginning of human history sexual relations were promiscuous; that therefore only the mother's parenthood was unquestionable, to her alone could consanguinity be traced, and she was the authority and lawgiver—the ruler both in the family group and in society. On the basis of his analysis of religious documents of Greek and Roman antiquity, Bachofen came to the conclusion that the supremacy of women had found its expression not only in the sphere of social and family organization but also in religion. He found evidence that the religion of the Olympian gods was preceded by a religion in which goddesses, motherlike figures, were the supreme deities.

Bachofen assumed that in a long-drawn-out historical process men defeated women, subdued them, and succeeded in making themselves the rulers in a social hierarchy. The patriarchal system thus established is characterized by monogamy (at least so far as women are concerned), by the authority of the father in the family, and by the dominant role of men in a hierarchically organized society. The religion of this patriarchal culture corresponded to its social organization. Instead of the mother-goddesses, male gods became supreme rulers over man, as the father was the supreme ruler in the family.

One of the most striking and brilliant illustrations of Bachofen's interpretation of Greek myths is his analysis of Aeschylus's *Oresteia*, which according to him, is a symbolic representation of a last fight between the maternal goddesses and the victorious paternal gods. Clytemnestra had killed her husband, Agamemnon, in order not to give up her lover, Aegisthus. Orestes, her son by Agamemnon, avenges his father's death by killing his mother and her lover. The Erinyes, representatives of the old mother-goddesses and the matriarchal principle, persecute Orestes and demand his punishment, while Apollo and Athene (the latter not born from woman but sprung from the head of Zeus), the representatives of the new patriarchal religion, are on Orestes' side. The argument is centered around the principles of patriarchal and matriarchal religion, respectively. For the matriarchal world there is only one sacred tie, that of mother and child, and consequently matricide is the ultimate and unforgivable crime. From the patriarchal point of view, the son's love and respect for the father is his paramount duty and therefore patricide is the paramount crime. Clytemnestra's killing of her husband, from the patriarchal standpoint a major crime because of the supreme position of the husband, is considered differently from the matriarchal standpoint, since "she was not related by blood to the man whom she killed." The murder of a husband does not concern the Erinyes, since to them only ties of blood and the sanctity of the mother count. To the Olympian gods, on the other hand, the murder of the mother is no crime if it is carried out as revenge for the father's death. In Aeschylus's *Oresteia*, Orestes is acquitted, but this victory of the patriarchal principle is somewhat mitigated by a compromise with the defeated goddesses. They agree to accept the new order and to be satisfied with a minor role as protectors of the earth and as goddesses of agricultural fertility.

Bachofen showed that the difference between the patriarchal and the matriarchal order went far beyond the social supremacy of men and women, respectively, but was one of social and moral principles. Matriarchal culture is characterized by an emphasis on ties of blood, ties to the soil, and a passive acceptance of all natural phenomena. Patriarchal society, in contrast, is characterized by respect for man-made law, by a predominance of rational thought, and by man's effort to change natural phenomena. In so far as these principles are concerned, the patriarchal culture constitutes a definite progress over the matriarchal world. In other respects, however, the matriarchal principles were superior to the victorious patriarchal ones. In the matriarchal concept all men are equal, since they are all the children of mothers and each one a child of Mother Earth. A mother loves all her children alike and without conditions, since her love is based on the fact that they are her children and not on any particular merit or achievement; the aim of life is the happiness of men, and there is nothing more important or dignified than human existence and life. The patriarchal system, on the other hand, considers obedience to authority to be the main virtue. Instead of the principle of equality, we find the concept of the favorite son and a hierarchical order in society.

> The relationship (Bachofen says) through which mankind has first grown into civilization which is the beginning of the development of every virtue and of the formation of the nobler aspects of human existence is the matriarchal principle, which becomes effective as the principle of love, unity, and peace. The woman sooner than the man learns in caring for the infant to extend her love beyond her own self to other human beings and to direct all her gifts and imagination to the aim of preserving and beautifying the existence of another being. All development of civilization, devotion, care, and the mourning for the dead are rooted in her.[6]
>
> The motherly love is not only more tender but also more general and universal. . . . Its principle is that of universality, whereas the patriarchal principle is that of restrictions . . . The idea of the universal brotherhood of man is rooted in the principle of motherhood, and this very idea vanishes with the development of patriarchal society. The patriarchal family is a closed and restricted organism. The matriarchal family, on

---

[6] J. J. Bachofen, *Der Mythus von Orient und Okzident,* edited by Manfred Schroeder (Munich: Ch. Becksche Buchhandlung, 1926), pp. 14 f.

the other hand, has that universal character with which all evolution begins and which is characteristic of maternal life in contrast to the spiritual, the image of Mother Earth, Demeter. Each woman's womb will give brothers and sisters to every human being until, with the development of the patriarchal principle, this unity is dissolved and superseded by the principle of hierarchy. In matriarchal societies, this principle has found frequent and even legally formulated expressions. It is the basis of the principle of universal freedom and equality which we find as one of the basic traits in matriarchal cultures. . . . Absence of inner disharmony, a longing for peace . . . a tender humaneness which one can still see in the facial expression of Egyptian statues penetrates the matriarchal world. . . .[7]

Bachofen's discovery found confirmation by an American scholar, L. H. Morgan, who entirely independently came to the conclusion[8] that the kinship system of the American Indians— similar to that found in Asia, Africa, and Australia—was based on the matriarchal principle and that the most significant institution in such cultures, the gens, was organized in conformity with the matriarchal principle. Morgan's conclusion about principles of value in a matriarchal society were quite similar to Bachofen's. He proposed that the higher form of civilization "will be a repetition—but

[7] *Ibid.*, pp. 15, 18.
[8] Tentatively in his *Systems of Consanguinity and Affinity*, 1871, and more definitely in *Ancient Society* (Chicago: Charles H. Kerr & Co., 1877).

on a higher level—of the principles of liberty, equality, and fraternity which characterized the ancient gens." Both Bachofen's and Morgan's theories of matriarchy were, if not entirely ignored, disputed by most anthropologists. This was also the case in the work of Robert Briffault, who in *The Mothers*[9] continued Bachofen's research and confirmed it by a brilliant analysis of new anthropological data. The violence of the antagonism against the theory of matriarchy arouses the suspicion that the criticism was not entirely free from an emotionally founded prejudice against an assumption so foreign to the thinking and feeling of our patriarchal culture. There is little doubt that many single objections to the matriarchal theory are justified. Nevertheless, Bachofen's main thesis, that we find an older layer of matriarchal religion underneath the more recent patriarchal religion of Greece, seems to me to be established by him beyond any doubt.

After this brief survey of Bachofen's theory we are in a better position to take up the discussion of our hypothesis that the hostility between father and son, which is the theme running through Sophocles's trilogy, is to be understood as an attack against the victorious patriarchal order by the representatives of the defeated matriarchal system.

King Oedipus offers little direct evidence except in some points which will be mentioned presently. But the original Oedipus myth in the various versions which existed in Greece and upon which Sophocles built his tragedy gives an important clue. In the various formu-

[9] New York: The Macmillan Company, 1927.

lations of the myth, the figure of Oedipus was always connected with the cult of the earth-goddesses, the representatives of matriarchal religion. In almost all versions of the Oedipus myth, from parts which deal with his exposure as an infant to those which are centered around his death, traces of this connection can be found.[10] Thus, for instance, Eteonos, the only Boeotian city which had a cult shrine of Oedipus and where the whole myth probably originated, also has the shrine of the earth-goddess, Demeter.[11] At Colonus (near Athens), where Oedipus finds his last resting place, was an old shrine of Demeter and the Erinyes which had probably existed prior to the Oedipus myth.[12] As we shall see later, Sophocles has emphasized this connection between Oedipus and the chthonic goddesses in *Oedipus at Colonus*.

Another aspect of the Oedipus myth—Oedipus's connection with the Sphinx—seems also to point to the connection between Oedipus and the matriarchal principle as described by Bachofen. The Sphinx had announced that the one who could solve her riddle would save the city from her wrath. Oedipus succeeds, where everyone else before him had failed, and thus becomes the savior of Thebes. But if we look at the riddle more closely we are struck by the insignificance of the riddle in comparison with the reward for its solution. Any clever boy of twelve might guess that that which goes first on four, then on two, and eventually on three

---

[10] Cf. Schneidewin, "Die Sage vom Oedipus," in *Abhandlung der Gesenichte der W. z. Gott.*, V, 1852, p. 192.

[11] Cf. Carl Roberts, *op. cit.*, pp. 1 ff.

[12] *Ibid.*, p. 21.

is man. Why should the right guess be proof of such extraordinary powers as to make their possessor the savior of the city? The answer to this question lies in an analysis of the real meaning of the riddle, an analysis which must follow the principles of interpretation of myths and dreams as they were developed by Bachofen and Freud.[18] They have shown that often the most important element in the real content of a dream or myth appears as a much less important or even insignificant part of the manifest formulation, whereas that part of the manifest formulation which has the main accent is only a minor part in the real content.

Applying this principle to the Sphinx myth, it would seem that the important element in the riddle is not the part which is stressed in the manifest formulation of the myth, namely, the riddle itself, but the answer to the riddle, *man*. If we translate the Sphinx's words from symbolic into overt language, we hear her say: He who knows that the most important answer man can give to the most difficult question with which he is confronted is *man himself* can save mankind. The riddle itself, the answer to which required nothing but cleverness, serves only as a veil for the latent meaning of the question, the importance of man. This very emphasis on the importance of man is part of the principle of the matriarchal world as Bachofen described it. Sophocles, in *Antigone*, made this principle the cen-

[18] Their interpretation of the Sphinx myth, however, differs from the one which follows here. Bachofen emphasized the nature of the question and stated that the Sphinx defines man in terms of his telluric, material existence, that is, in matriarchal terms. Freud assumed the riddle to be the symbolic expression of the child's sexual curiosity.

ter of Antigone's as against Creon's position. What matters for Creon and the patriarchal order he represents is the state, man-made laws, and obedience to them. What matters to Antigone is man himself, the natural law, and love. Oedipus becomes the savior of Thebes, proving by his very answer to the Sphinx that he belongs to the same world which is represented by Antigone and expressive of the matriarchal order.

One element in the myth and in Sophocles's *King Oedipus* seems to contradict our hypothesis—the figure of Jocasta. On the assumption that she symbolizes the motherly principle, the question arises why the mother is destroyed instead of being victorious, provided the explanation suggested here is correct. The answer to this question will show that the role of Jocasta not only does not contradict our hypothesis but tends to confirm it. Jocasta's crime is that of not having fulfilled her duty as a mother; she had wanted to kill her child in order to save her husband. This, from the standpoint of patriarchal society, is a legitimate decision, but from the standpoint of matriarchal society and matriarchal ethics it is the unforgivable crime. It is she who by committing this crime starts the chain of events which eventually lead to her own and to her husband's and son's destruction. In order to understand this point, we must not lose sight of the fact that the myth as it was known to Sophocles had already been changed according to the patriarchal pattern, that the manifest and conscious frame of reference is that of patriarchy, and that the latent and older meaning appears only in a veiled and often distorted form. The patriarchal system had been victorious, and the myth explains the reasons for the downfall of matriarchy. It proposes that the mother by violating her paramount duty brought about her own destruction. The final judgment, however, whether this interpretation of Jocasta's role and of *King Oedipus* is correct must wait until we have analyzed *Oedipus at Colonus* and *Antigone*.

In *Oedipus at Colonus* we see the blind Oedipus accompanied by his two daughters arriving near Athens, close to the grove of the goddesses of the earth. The oracle has prophesied that, if Oedipus were to be buried in this grove, he would protect Athens from invasion by her enemies. In the course of the tragedy Oedipus makes known to Theseus the word of the oracle. Theseus gladly accepts the offer that Oedipus become the posthumous benefactor of Athens. Oedipus retreats into the grove of the goddesses and dies in a mysterious way not known to anybody but Theseus.

Who are these goddesses? Why do they offer a sanctuary to Oedipus? What does the oracle mean by telling us that Oedipus in finding his last home in this grove reverts to his role of savior and benefactor?

In *Oedipus at Colonus* Oedipus implores the goddesses, saying:

> *Queens of dread aspect,** since your seat is the first in this land whereat I have bent the knee, show not yourselves ungracious to Phoebus or to myself; who, when he proclaimed that doom of many woes, spake of this as a rest for me after long years—on reaching my

* Italics are the author's.

goal in a land where I should find a seat of the
*Awful Goddesses,** and a hospitable shelter
—even that there I should close my weary life,
with benefits, through my having dwelt
therein, for mine hosts, but ruin for those who
sent me forth—who drove me away.[14]

Oedipus calls the goddesses "Queens of dread aspect" and "Awful Goddesses." Why are they "dreadful"
and "awful," since to him they are the goddesses of his
last resting place and those who will give him peace
eventually? Why does the chorus say:

A wanderer that old man must have been
—a wanderer, not a dweller in the land; else
never would he have advanced into this un-
trodden *grove of the maidens* with whom
none may strive, *whose name we tremble to
speak,* by whom we pass with eyes turned
away, moving our lips, without sound or word,
in still devotion.[15]

The answer to this question can be found only in
that principle of interpretation, valid for both myths
and dreams, which has been recognized by Bachofen
and Freud. If an element appearing in a myth or in a
dream belongs to a much earlier phase of development
and is not part of the conscious frame of reference at
the time of the final formulation of the myth, this element often carries with it the quality of dread and

---

* Italics are the author's.
[14] Translation by R. C. Webb, in *The Complete Greek Drama*, cited
above.
[15] *Ibid.*

awfulness. Touching upon something hidden and ta-
boo, the conscious mind is affected by a fear of a particular kind—the fear of the unknown and the mysti-
fying.

Goethe, in one of the least understood passages of
Faust, has treated the problem of the dread of the mysterious mothers in a spirit very similar to that in Sophocles's *Oedipus at Colonus.* Mephistopheles says:

> Unwilling I reveal a loftier mystery—
> In solitude are throned the *Goddesses,*
> No space around them, Place and
>   Time still less;
> *Only to speak of them embarrasses;*
> *They are the Mothers!*

FAUST (terrified): Mothers!

MEPHISTOPHELES: *Hast thou dread?*

FAUST: The Mothers! Mothers!—a strange
    word is said.

MEPHISTOPHELES:

> It is so. Goddesses, unknown to ye,
> The Mothers, named by us so unwillingly.
> Delve in the deepest depth must thou, to
>   reach them:
> It is thine own fault that we for help beseech
>   them.

Here too, as in Sophocles's tragedy, the feeling of
dread and terror is bound up with the mere mentioning
of the goddesses, who belong to an ancient world which
now is banned from the light of day, from consciousness.

As we see from this short passage, Goethe anticipated Bachofen's theory; according to Eckermann's diary (January 10, 1830), Goethe mentioned that in reading Plutarch he found "that in Grecian antiquity the Mothers are spoken of as Goddesses." This passage in *Faust* has appeared enigmatic to most commentators who tried to explain the mothers as a symbol of Platonic ideas, the formless realm of the inner world of spirit, and so forth. Indeed, it must remain an enigma unless one understands it in the light of Bachofen's findings.

It is in the grove of these "awful" goddesses where Oedipus, the wanderer, at last comes to rest and finds his real home. Oedipus, although himself a man, belongs to the world of these matriarchal goddesses, and his strength lies in his connection with them.

Oedipus's return to the grove of the goddesses, though the most important, is not the only clue to the understanding of his position as representative of the matriarchal order. Sophocles makes another and very plain allusion to matriarchy by having Oedipus refer to Egyptian matriarchy[16] when he tells about his two daughters. This is the way he praises them:

> O true image of the *ways of Egypt that they show in their spirit and their life! For there the men sit weaving in the house, but the wives go forth to win the daily bread*. And in your case, my daughters, those to whom these toils belonged keep the house at home

[16] Sophocles probably refers here to a passage from *Herodotus*, II, 35.

like girls, while ye, in their stead, bear your
hapless father's burden.[17]

The same trend of thought is continued by Oedipus when he compares his daughters with his sons. Of
Antigone and Ismene he says:

> Now, these girls preserve me, these my
> nurses, *these who are men not women,* in true
> service: but ye are aliens, and no sons of
> mine.[18]

We have raised the question whether, if incest was
the essence of Oedipus's crime, the drama should have
told us that he had fallen in love with Jocasta unwittingly. In *Oedipus at Colonus,* Sophocles has Oedipus
himself answer this question. The marriage to her was
not the outcome of his own desire and decision; instead,
she was one of the rewards for the city's savior.

> Thebes bound me, all unknowingly, to
> the bride that was my curse.[19]

We have already pointed to the fact that the main
theme of the trilogy, the conflict between father and
son, finds its full expression in *Oedipus at Colonus;*
here the hate between father and son is not, as in *King
Oedipus,* unconscious; indeed, here Oedipus is very
much aware of his hate against his sons, whom he accuses of having violated the eternal law of nature. He
claims that his curse is stronger than the sons' prayer to

[17] Webb, *op. cit.*
[18] *Ibid.*
[19] *Ibid*

Poseidon, "if indeed Justice (Dike, the *Goddess* of Justice, who protects the eternal law of natural bonds and not the man-made rights of the first-born son), revealed of old, sits with Zeus in the might of eternal laws." [20] Simultaneously he gives expression to his hate against his own parents, accusing them of their intention to sacrifice his life. There is no indication in *Oedipus at Colonus* that the hostility of Oedipus's sons against their father has any connection with the incest motif. The only motivation we can find in the tragedy is their wish for power and the rivalry with their father.

The end of *Oedipus at Colonus* clarifies still further the meaning of Oedipus's connection with the goddesses of the earth.

After the chorus has prayed to the "Unseen Goddesses," "the Goddess Infernal," the messenger reports how Oedipus died. He has taken leave of his daughters and—accompanied only, though not guided, by Theseus—walks to the holy place of the goddesses. He seems to need no guidance, since here at last he is at home and knows his way. The messenger sees Theseus

> . . . holding his hand before his face to screen his eyes, as if *some dread sight had been seen,* and such as none might endure to behold. [21]

We find here again the emphasis on something awful and terrifying. The line following the ones just quoted makes it very clear how the remnants of the

[20] *Ibid.*
[21] *Ibid.*

matriarchal religion are blended with the ruling patriarchal system. The messenger reports that he saw Theseus

> . . . salute the earth and the home of the gods above, both at once, in one prayer.[22]

The end of the description of Oedipus's death shows the same blend of the patriarchal and matriarchal systems. The messenger goes on:

> But by what doom Oedipus perished, no man can tell, save Theseus alone. No fiery thunderbolt of the god removed him in that hour, nor any rising of storm from the sea; but either a messenger from the gods, *or the world of the dead, the nether adamant, riven for him in love,* without pain; for the passing of the man was not with lamentation, or in sickness and suffering, but, above mortal's wonderful. And if to any I seem to speak folly, I would not woo their belief, who count me foolish.[23]

The messenger is puzzled; he does not know whether Oedipus was removed from the earth by the gods above or by the gods below, by the world of the fathers or that of the mothers. But we can be certain that, in a formulation written centuries after the mother-goddesses had been conquered by the Olympian gods, this doubt can only be the expression of a secret con-

[22] *Ibid.*
[23] *Ibid.*

viction that Oedipus was brought back to the place where he belonged, to the mothers.

How different is the end of *Oedipus at Colonus* from that of *King Oedipus*. In the latter, his fate seemed to be sealed as that of the tragic criminal whose crime removes him forever from his family and from his fellow men, destined to be an outcast, abhorred though perhaps pitied by everyone. In the former he dies as a man surrounded by two loving daughters and by new friends whose benefactor he has become, not with a feeling of guilt but with a conviction of his right, not as an outcast but as one who has eventually found his home—with the earth and the goddesses who rule there. The tragic guilt that had pervaded *King Oedipus* has now been removed, and only one conflict has remained as bitter and unsolved as ever—that between father and son.

The conflict between the patriarchal and matriarchal principles is the theme of the third part of the trilogy, *Antigone*. Here the figure of Creon, which has been somewhat indistinct in the two former tragedies, becomes colorful and definite. He has become the tyrant of Thebes after Oedipus's two sons have been killed—one by attacking the city in order to gain power, the other defending his throne. Creon has ordered that the legitimate king should be buried and that the challenger's body should be left unburied—the greatest humiliation and dishonor to be done to a man, according to Greek custom. The principle that Creon represents is that of the supremacy of the law of the state over ties of blood, of obedience to authority over allegiance to the natural law of humanity. Antigone refuses to violate the laws of blood and of the solidarity of all human beings for the sake of an authoritarian, hierarchical principle.

The two principles for which Creon and Antigone stand are those which Bachofen characterized as the patriarchal as against the matriarchal principle, respectively. The matriarchal principle is that of blood relationship as the fundamental and indestructible tie, of the equality of all men, of the respect for human life and of love. The patriarchal principle is that the ties between man and wife, between ruler and ruled, take precedence over ties of blood. It is the principle of order and authority, of obedience and hierarchy.

Antigone represents the matriarchal principle and thus is the uncompromising adversary of the representative of patriarchal authority, Creon. Ismene, in constrast, has accepted the defeat and given in to the victorious patriarchal order; she is a symbol of women under patriarchal domination. Sophocles makes her role very clear by having her say to Antigone, who has decided to defy Creon's command:

> And now *we* in turn—we two left all alone—think how we shall perish, more miserably than all the rest, if, in defiance of the law, we brave a king's decree or his powers. Nay, we must remember, first, *that we were born women, as who should not strive with men;* next, that we are ruled of the stronger, so that we must obey in these things, and in things yet sorer. I, therefore, asking

the *Spirits Infernal* to pardon, seeing that force is put on me herein, will hearken to our rulers; for 'tis witless to be over busy.[24]

Ismene has accepted male authority as her ultimate norm; she has accepted the defeat of women "who should not strive with men." Her loyalty to the goddesses is expressed only in begging them to forgive her who has to yield to the force of the ruler.

The humanistic principle of the matriarchal world, with its emphasis on man's greatness and dignity, finds a beautiful and forceful expression in the chorus's praise of the power of man:

> Wonders are many, *and none is more wonderful than man;* the power that crosses the white sea, driven by the stormy southwind, making a path under surges that threaten to engulf him; and *Earth, the eldest of the gods,* the immortal, the unwearied, doth he wear, turning the soil with the offspring of horses, as the ploughs go to and fro from year to year.[25]

The conflict between the two principles unfolds in the further development of the play. Antigone insists that the law she obeys is not that of the Olympian gods. Her law "is not of today or yesterday, but from all time, and no man knows when they were first put forth";[26] and, we may add, the law of burial, of returning the body to Mother Earth, is rooted in the very principles

[24] *Ibid.*
[25] *Ibid.*
[26] *Ibid.*

of matriarchal religion. Antigone stands for the solidarity of man and the principle of the all-embracing motherly love. "'Tis not my nature to join in hating but in loving." [27]

For Creon, obedience to authority is the supreme value; human solidarity and love, if in conflict with obedience, have to yield. He has to defeat Antigone in order to uphold patriarchal authority and with it his virility.

> Now verily I am no man, she is the man,
> if this victory shall rest with her, and bring no penalty.[28]

Creon lays down the authoritarian, patriarchal principle in unequivocal language:

> Yea, this, my son, should be thy heart's fixed law—in all things to *obey thy father's will*. 'Tis for this that men pray to see *dutiful children* grow up around them in their homes —that such may requite their father's foe with evil, and honour, as their father doth, his friend. But he who *begets unprofitable children*—what shall we say that he hath sown, but trouble for himself, and much triumph for his foes? Then do not thou, my son, at pleasure's beck, dethrone thy reason for a woman's sake; knowing that this is a joy that soon grows cold in clasping arms—an evil woman to share thy bed and thy home. For what wound could strike deeper than a false

---

[27] *Ibid.*
[28] *Ibid.*

friend? Nay, with loathing, and as if she were thine enemy, let this girl go to find a husband in the house of Hades. For since I have taken her, alone of all the city, in open disobedience, I will not make myself a liar to my people—I will slay her.

So let her appeal as she will to the majesty of kindred blood. If I am to nurture mine own kindred in naughtiness, needs must I bear with it in aliens. *He who does his duty in his own household will be found righteous in the State also. But if any one transgresses and does violence to the laws, or thinks to dictate to his rulers, such a one can win no praise from me. No, whomsoever the city may appoint, that man must be obeyed, in little things and great, in just things and unjust; and I should feel sure that one who thus obeys would be a good ruler no less than a good subject,* and in the storm of spears would stand his ground where he was set, loyal and dauntless at his comrade's side.

But disobedience is the worst of evils. This it is that ruins cities; this makes home desolate; by this, the ranks of allies are broken into headlong rout; but, of the lives whose course is fair, the greater part owes safety to obedience. *Therefore, we must support the cause of order, and in no wise suffer a woman to worst us. Better to fall from power, if we must, by a man's hand; than we should be called weaker than a woman.*[29]

* *Ibid.*

Authority in the family and authority in the state are the two interrelated supreme values for which Creon stands. Sons are the property of their fathers and their function is to be "serviceable" to the father. "Pater potestas" in the family is the basis for the ruler's power in the state. Citizens are the property of the state and its ruler, and "disobedience is the worst of evils."

Haemon, Creon's son, represents the principles for which Antigone fights. Although he tries at first to appease and persuade his father, he declares his opposition openly when he sees that his father will not yield. He relies on reason, "the highest of all things that we call our own" and on the will of the people. When Creon accuses Antigone of being tainted with the "malady of disobedience," Haemon's rebellious answer is:

"Our Theban folk, with one voice, denies it." [30]

When Creon argues:

Am I to rule this land by other judgment than mine own?

Haemon's answer is:

That is no city which belongs to one man.
Thou wouldst make a good monarch of a desert.[31]

Creon brings the argument again to the crucial point by saying:

"This boy, it seems, is the *woman's* champion."

[30] *Ibid.*
[31] *Ibid.*

And Haemon points to the matriarchal goddesses by answering: "And for thee, and for me, and for *the gods below.*" [32]

The two principles have now been stated with full clarity, and the end of the tragedy only carries the action to the point of final decision. Creon has Antigone buried alive in a cave—again a symbolic expression of her connection with the goddesses of the earth. The seer, Theiresias, who in *King Oedipus* was instrumental in making Oedipus aware of his crime, appears again, this time to make Creon aware of his. Stricken by panic, Creon gives in and tries to save Antigone. He rushes to the cave where she is entombed, but Antigone is already dead. Haemon tries to kill his father; when he fails, he takes his own life. Creon's wife, Erydice, upon hearing the fate of her son, kills herself, cursing her husband as the murderer of her children. Creon recognizes the complete collapse of his world and the defeat of his principles. He admits his own moral bankruptcy, and the play ends with his confession:

> Ah me, this guilt can never be fixed on any other mortal kind, for my acquittal! I, even I, was thy slayer, wretched that I am— I own the truth. Lead me away, O my servants, lead me hence with all speed, whose life is but as death! . . .
>
> Lead me away, I pray you; a rash, foolish man; who have slain thee, ah, my son, unwittingly, and thee, too, my wife—unhappy that I am! I know not which way I should bend my

[32] *Ibid.*

gaze, or where I should seek support; for all
is amiss with that which is in my hands,—and
yonder again, a crushing fate hath leapt upon
my head.[33]

We are now in a position to answer the questions
we raised at the beginning. Is the Oedipus myth as
presented in Sophocles's trilogy centered around the
crime of incest? Is the murder of the father the symbolic expression of a hate resulting from jealousy?
Though the answer is doubtful at the end of *King Oedipus,* it is hardly doubtful any more at the end of *Antigone.* Not Oedipus but Creon is defeated in the end,
and with him the principle of authoritarianism, of
man's domination over men, the father's domination
over his son, and the dictator's domination over the people. If we accept the theory of matriarchal forms of society and religion, then, indeed, there seems to be little
doubt that Oedipus, Haemon, and Antigone are representatives of the old principles of matriarchy, those of
equality and democracy, in contrast to Creon, who represents patriarchal domination and obedience.[34]

[33] *Ibid.*
[34] No less a thinker than Hegal saw the conflict represented in Antigone in the same light many years prior to Bachofen. He says of
Antigone: "The gods, however, which she worships are the gods below, the gods of Hades, the inner gods of emotion, of love, of blood,
and not the gods of the day, of the free and self-conscious life, of the
nation, and the state." (Hegel, *Aesthetik,* II, 2, Absch., Ch. I; compare
also *Philosophy of Religion,* XVI, p. 133). Hegel in this statement is
so much on the side of the state and its laws that he defines Creon's
principle as that of "the free life of the people and the state" in spite
of the undeniable evidence that Creon does not represent freedom
but dictatorship. In view of this one-sided sympathy of Hegel's, it is
all the more significant that he states so clearly that Antigone stands
for the principles of love, of blood and emotion, which later on

Our interpretation, however, needs to be supplemented by another consideration. Although the conflict between Oedipus, Antigone and Haemon, on the one side, against Creon, on the other, contains a memory of the conflict between patriarchal and matriarchal principles, and particularly of its mythical elements, it must also be understood in terms of the specific political and cultural situation in Sophocles's time and of his reactions to that situation.

Bachofen found to be the characteristic principles of the matriarchal world. While Hegel's sympathy for the patriarchal principles is not surprising, one does not expect to find it in Bachofen's writings. And yet Bachofen's own attitude to matriarchal society has been quite ambivalent. It seems that he loved matriarchate and hated patriarchal principles, but inasmuch as he was also a religious Protestant and a believer in the progress of reason, he believed in the supremacy of the patriarchal principle over matriarchate. In a great part of his writings his sympathy with the matriarchal principle finds expression. In other parts, and this holds true of his brief interpretation of the Oedipus myth (Bachofen's "Mutterrecht" in *Der Mythos vom Orient und Okzident*, cited above, pp. 259 f.), he, like Hegel, sides with the victorious Olympian gods. To him Oedipus stands on the frontier between the matriarchal and the patriarchal world. The fact that he does not know his father points to a matriarchal origin in which only the mother but not the father is certain. But the fact that he discovers eventually who his real father is, according to Bachofen, marks the beginning of the patriarchal family in which the true father is known. "Oedipus," he says, "is connected with the progress to a higher level of existence. He is one of those great figures whose suffering and pain lead to a more beautiful form of human civilization; one of those still rooted in the old order of things who are at the same time sacrificed and thus become the founders of a new epoch" (p. 266). Bachofen stresses the fact that the dreaded mother-goddesses, the Erinyes, have subordinated themselves to the Apollonian world and that the connection between Oedipus and them marks the victory of the patriarchal principle. It seems to me that Bachofen's interpretation does not do justice to the fact that Creon, although he is the only one who survives physically, symbolizing the victory of the patriarchal world, is the one who is morally defeated. It may be assumed that Sophocles intended to convey the idea that the patriarchal world was triumphant, but that it would be defeated unless it adopted the humanistic principles of the older matriarchal order.

The Peloponnesian war, the threat to the political independence of Athens, and the plague that ravaged the city at the beginning of the war had helped to uproot the old religious and philosophical traditions. Indeed, attacks against religion were not new, but they reached a climax in the teachings of Sophocles's Sophist adversaries. He was opposed particularly to those Sophists who not only proclaimed despotism exercised by an intellectual elite but also upheld unrestricted selfishness as a moral principle. The ethics of egotistical supermen proclaimed by this wing of the Sophists and their amoral opportunism were the very opposite of Sophocles's philosophy. In Creon, Sophocles created a figure representing this school of sophism, and Creon's speeches resembled the Sophist pattern even in style and expression.[35]

In his argument against the Sophists, Sophocles gave new expression to the old religious traditions of the people with their emphasis on love, equality, and justice. "The religious attitude of Sophocles. . . . is primarily concerned not with the official religion of the state but with those helpful secondary powers which always were closer to the faith of the masses than the aristocratic Olympians and to whom the people turned again in the dangers of the Peloponnesian war."[36] These "secondary powers," which were different from the "aristocratic Olympian" gods, are easily identified as the goddesses of the matriarchal world.

[35] Cf. Callicles in Plato's *Georgias* and Thrasymachus in his *Republic*.
[36] Wilhelm Schmid, "Geschicte der Griechischen Literatur," 1. Teil, in *Handbuch der Altertumswissenschaften*, edited by Walter Otto, J. Abt., 1. Teil, 2. Band (Munich, 1934).

We see, then, that Sophocles's views, expressed in the Oedipus trilogy, are to be understood as a blend of his opposition to contemporary sophism and of his sympathy for the old, non-Olympian religious ideas.[37] In the name of both he proclaimed the principle that the dignity of man and the sanctity of human bonds must never be subordinated to inhuman and authoritarian claims of the state or to opportunistic considerations.[38]

2. The Myth of Creation

The Babylonian myth of Creation (Enuma Elish) tells us of a victorious rebellion of male gods against Tiamat, the great mother who ruled the universe. They form an alliance against her and choose Marduk to be their leader in this fight. After a bitter war Tiamat is slain, from her body heaven and earth are formed, and Marduk rules as supreme God.

However, before he is chosen to be the leader, Marduk has to pass a test, which seems insignificant and puzzling in the context of the whole story and yet which, as I shall try to show, is the key to the understanding of the myth. This is the description of the test:

[37] It is interesting to note that the same blend between progressive political ideas and a sympathy with mythical matriarchal principles is to be found again in the nineteenth century in Bachofen's, Engel's and Morgan's work. (Compare my paper on "Zur Rezeption der Mutterrechtstheorie" in Zeitschrift fuer Sozialforschung, III [1934].)
[38] Cf. also Wilhelm Nestle, "Sophokles und die Sophistik," Classical Philology (Chicago: University of Chicago Press, 1910), Vol. 5, II, pp. 129 ff.

The problem of hostility between father and son was also of great personal significance in the life of the poet. Jophon, the son, sued his aged father and wanted the court to deprive him of the right to manage his own business affairs, a suit from which Sophocles emerged victorious.

Then they placed a garment in their
    midst;
To Marduk, their first-born, they said:
"Verily, O lord, thy destiny is supreme
    among the gods,
Command 'to destroy and to create,'
    (and) it shall be!
By the word of thy mouth let the garment
    be destroyed;
Command again, and let the garment be
    whole!"
He commanded with his mouth, and the
    garment was destroyed.
Again he commanded, and the garment
    was restored.
When the gods, his fathers, beheld the
    efficiency of his word,
They rejoiced (and) did homage, (say-
    ing) "Marduk is king!" [39]

What is the significance of this test? Does it not
sound like a trivial bit of magic rather than the crucial
test that is to determine whether Marduk will be able
to defeat Tiamat?

In order to understand the meaning of the test, we
must remember what has been said of the problem of
matriarchy in the discussion of the Oedipus myth. Quite
clearly the Babylonian myth reports the conflict
between patriarchal and matriarchal principles of social
organization and of religious orientation. The rule of

[39] Quoted from Alexander Heidel, *The Babylonian Genesis*, (Chicago:
University of Chicago Press, 1942), ENUMA ELISH (When Above),
Tablet IV.

the great Mother is challenged by the male sons. But how can they win when they are inferior to women in one essential aspect? Women have the gift of natural creation, they can bear children. Men are sterile in this respect. (That the male sperm is as indispensable for the formation of the child as the female egg is true enough, but this knowledge is rather on the level of a scientific statement than on that of an obvious recognizable fact like pregnancy or childbirth. Moreover, the father's part in the creation of the child is terminated with the act of impregnation when the mother's role in bearing the child, then giving birth to it and nursing it begins.) Quite in contrast to Freud's assumption that the "penis envy" is a natural phenomenon in the constitution of the woman's psyche, there are good reasons for assuming that before male supremacy was established there was a "pregnancy envy" in the man, which even today can be found in numerous cases. In order to defeat the mother, the male must prove that he is not inferior, that he has the gift to produce. Since he cannot produce with a womb, he must produce in another fashion; he produces with his mouth, his word, his thought. This, then, is the meaning of the test: Marduk can defeat Tiamat only if he can prove that he can also create even though in a different fashion. The test shows us the deep male-female antagonism, which is the basis of the fight between Tiamat and Marduk and the essential point of contention in this fight between the two sexes. With Marduk's victory male supremacy is established, the natural productiveness of the women is devaluated, and the male begins his domination based on his ability to produce by the power of thought, a form of production which underlies the development of human civilization.

The Biblical myth begins where the Babylonian myth has ended. The supremacy of a male god is established and hardly any trace of a previous matriarchal stage is left. Marduk's "test" has become the main theme of the Biblical story of Creation. God creates the world by his word; the woman and her creative powers are no longer necessary. Even the natural course of events, that women give birth to men, is reversed. Eve is born from Adam's rib (like Athene from Zeus's head). The elimination of every memory of matriarchal supremacy is, though, not entirely complete. In the figure of Eve we see the woman who is superior to the male. She takes the initiative in eating the forbidden fruit; she does not consult with Adam, she simply gives him the fruit to eat and he, when discovered, is rather clumsy and inept in his excuses. It is only after the Fall that his domination is established. God says to Eve: "And thy desire shall be to thy husband and he shall rule over thee." Quite obviously this establishment of male domination points to a previous situation in which he did not rule. Only from this and from the complete negation of the productive role of the woman can we recognize the traces of an underlying theme of the dominant role of the mother, which is still part of the manifest text in the Babylonian myth.

This myth offers a good illustration of the mechanism of distortion and censorship that plays such a prominent role in Freud's interpretation of dreams and myths. Memories of older social and religious principles are still contained in the Biblical myth. But at the time of its composition as we know it now, these older principles were so much in contrast to the prevailing thought that they could not be made explicit. And now we recognize traces of the former system only in small details,[40] over-reactions, inconsistencies, and the connection of the later myth with older variations of the same theme.

3. *Little Red-Cap*

Little Red-Cap is a good illustration of Freud's views while at the same time offering a variation of the theme of the male-female conflict that we found in the Oedipus trilogy and in the myth of Creation. This is the fairy tale:

> Once upon a time there was a dear little girl who was loved by everyone who looked at her, but most of all by her grandmother, and there was nothing that she would not have given to the child. Once she gave her a *little cap of red velvet*, which suited her so well that she would never wear anything else; so she was always called "Little Red-Cap."
>
> One day her mother said to her: "Come, Little Red-Cap, here is a piece of cake and a bottle of wine; take them to your grandmother, she is ill and weak, and they will do her good. Set out before it gets hot, and when

[40] The Babylonian Tiamat probably appears in the Biblical story is the "Tehom," the deep upon whose face is darkness."

you are going, walk nicely and quietly and do not run off the path, or you may fall and break the bottle, and then your grandmother will get nothing; and when you go into her room, don't forget to say, 'Good-morning,' and don't peep into every corner before you do it."

"I will take great care," said Little Red-Cap to her mother, and gave her hand on it.

The grandmother lived out in the wood, half a league from the village, and just as Little Red-Cap entered the wood, a wolf met her. Red-Cap did not know what a wicked creature he was, and was not at all afraid of him.

"Good-day, Little Red-Cap," said he

"Thank you kindly, wolf."

"Whither away so early, Little Red-Cap?"

"To my grandmother's."

"What have you got in your apron?"

"Cake and wine; yesterday was baking-day, so poor sick grandmother is to have something good, to make her stronger."

"Where does your grandmother live, Little Red-Cap?"

"A good quarter of a league farther on in the wood; her house stands under the three large oak-trees, the nut-trees are just below; you must surely know it," replied Little Red-Cap.

The wolf thought to himself: "What a tender young creature! what a nice plump mouthful—she will be better to eat than the old woman. I must act craftily, so as to catch both." So he walked for a short time by the side of Little Red-Cap, and then he said: "See, Little Red-Cap, how pretty the flowers are about here—why do you not look around? I believe, too, that you do not hear how sweetly the little birds are singing; you walk gravely along as if you were going to school, while everything else out here in the wood is merry."

Little Red-Cap raised her eyes, and when she saw the sunbeams dancing here and there through the trees, and pretty flowers growing everywhere, she thought: "Suppose I take grandmother a fresh nosegay; that would please her too. It is so early in the day that I shall still get there in good time"; and so she ran from the path into the wood to look for flowers. And whenever she picked one, she fancied that she saw a still prettier one farther on, and ran after it, and so got deeper and deeper into the wood.

Meanwhile the wolf ran straight to the grandmother's house and knocked at the door.

"Who is there?"

"Little Red-Cap," replied the wolf. "She is bringing cake and wine; open the door."

"Lift the latch," called out the grandmother, "I am too weak, and cannot get up."

The wolf lifted the latch, the door sprang open, and without saying a word he went straight to the grandmother's bed, and devoured her. Then he put on her clothes, dressed himself in her cap, laid himself in bed and drew the curtains.

Little Red-Cap, however, had been running about picking flowers, and when she had gathered so many that she could carry no more, she remembered her grandmother, and set out on the way to her.

She was surprised to find the cottage-door standing open, and when she went into the room, she had such a strange feeling that she said to herself: "Oh dear! how uneasy I feel today, and at other times I like being with grandmother so much." She called out: "Good morning," but received no answer; so she went to the bed and drew back the curtains. There lay her grandmother with her cap pulled over her face, and looking very strange.

"Oh grandmother," she said, "what big ears you have!"

"The better to hear you with, my child," was the reply.

"But, grandmother, what big eyes you have!" she said.

"The better to see you with, my dear."

"But, grandmother, what large hands you have!"

"The better to hug you with."

"Oh! but, grandmother, what a terrible big mouth you have!"

"The better to eat you with!"

And scarcely had the wolf said this, than with one bound he was out of bed and swallowed up Red-Cap.

When the wolf had appeased his appetite, he lay down again in the bed, fell asleep and began to snore very loud. The huntsman was just passing the house, and thought to himself: "How the old woman is snoring! I must just see if she wants anything." So he went into the room, and when he came to the bed, he saw that the wolf was lying in it. "Do I find you here, you old sinner!" said he. "I have long sought you!" Then just as he was going to fire at him, it occurred to him that the wolf might have devoured the grandmother, and that she might still be saved, so he did not fire, but took a pair of scissors, and began to cut open the stomach of the sleeping wolf. When he had made two snips, he saw the little red cap shining, and then he made two snips more, and the little girl sprang out, crying: "Ah, how frightened I have been! How dark it was inside the wolf"; and after that the aged grandmother came out alive also, but scarcely able to breathe. Red-Cap however, quickly fetched great stones with which they filled the wolf's belly, and when he awoke, he wanted to run away, but the stones were so heavy that he collapsed at once, and fell dead.

Then all three were delighted. The huntsman drew off the wolf's skin and went home with it; the grandmother ate the cake and drank the wine which Red-Cap had brought, and revived, but Red-Cap thought to herself: "As long as I live, I will never by myself leave the path, to run into the wood, when my mother has forbidden me to do so."

Most of the symbolism in this fairy tale can be understood without difficulty. The "little cap of red velvet" is a symbol of menstruation. The little girl of whose adventures we hear has become a mature woman and is now confronted with the problem of sex.

The warning "not to run off the path" so as not "to fall and break the bottle" is clearly a warning against the danger of sex and of losing her virginity.

The wolf's sexual appetite is aroused by the sight of the girl and he tries to seduce her by suggesting that she "look around and hear how sweetly the birds are singing." Little Red-Cap "raises her eyes" and following the wolf's suggestion she gets "deeper and deeper into the wood." She does so with a characteristic piece of rationalization: in order to convince herself that there is nothing wrong she reasons that grandmother would be happy with the flowers she might bring her.

But this deviation from the straight path of virtue is punished severely. The wolf, masquerading as the grandmother, swallows innocent Little Red-Cap. When he has appeased his appetite, he falls asleep.

So far the fairy tale seems to have one simple, moralistic theme, the danger of sex. But it is more complicated than that. What is the role of the man, and how is sex represented?

The male is portrayed as a ruthless and cunning animal, and the sexual act is described as a cannibalistic act in which the male devours the female. This view is not held by women who like men and enjoy sex. It is an expression of a deep antagonism against men and sex. But the hate and prejudice against men are even more clearly exhibited at the end of the story. Again, as in the Babylonian myth, we must remember that the woman's superiority consists in her ability to bear children. How, then, is the wolf made ridiculous? By showing that he attempted to play the role of a pregnant woman, having living beings in his belly. Little Red-Cap puts stones, a symbol of sterility, into his belly, and the wolf collapses and dies. His deed, according to the primitive law of retaliation, is punished according to his crime: he is killed by the stones, the symbol of sterility, which mock his usurpation of the pregnant woman's role.

This fairy tale, in which the main figures are three generations of women (the huntsman at the end is the conventional father figure without real weight), speaks of the male-female conflict; it is a story of triumph by man-hating women, ending with their victory, exactly the opposite of the Oedipus myth, which lets the male emerge victorious from this battle.

4. *The Sabbath Ritual*

Symbols, as we have dealt with them thus far, are pictorial images or words standing for an idea, feeling or thought. But there is still another kind of symbol, whose significance in the history of man is hardly less great than that of the symbols that occur in dreams, myths or fairy tales. I refer to the symbolic ritual where an action, and not a word or image, stands for an inner experience. We all use such symbolic rituals in our everyday life. If we take off our hat as a sign of respect, if we bow our head as a sign of deference, if we shake hands as an expression of friendly feelings we act—rather than speak—symbolically. Such symbols as the ones just mentioned are simple and easily understood; just as some dreams are clear to everyone without further elaboration. There are also many religious symbols which are equally simple; for instance, the old Hebrew custom of rending one's clothes as a sign of mourning. There are many other rituals, however, like the Sabbath ritual, which are as complicated—and in need of interpretation—as the symbolic language in dreams and in myths.

The rules for Sabbath observance have a prominent place in the Old Testament; this is, in fact, the only command referring to a ritual that is mentioned in the Ten Commandments. "Remember the sabbath day, to keep it holy. Six days shalt thou labour, and do all thy work: But the seventh day is the sabbath of the Lord thy God; in it thou shalt not do any work, thou, nor thy son, nor thy daughter, thy manservant, nor thy maidservant, nor thy cattle, nor thy stranger that is within thy gates: For in six days the Lord made heaven and earth, the sea, and all that in them is, and rested the seventh day: wherefore the Lord blessed the sabbath day, and hallowed it." (Ex. 20:8-11). In the second version of the Ten Commandments (Deut. 5:12-15) the observance of the Sabbath is commanded again, although here reference is not made to God's rest on the seventh day but to the exodus from Egypt: "And remember that thou wast a servant in the land of Egypt, and that the Lord thy God brought thee out thence through a mighty hand and by a stretched out arm: therefore the Lord thy God commanded thee to keep the sabbath day."

To the modern mind, there is not much of a problem in the Sabbath institution. The idea that man should rest from his work one day every week sounds to us like a self-evident, social-hygienic measure intended to give man the physical and spiritual rest and relaxation he needs in order not to be swallowed up by his daily work. No doubt, this explanation is true as far as it goes—but it does not answer some questions which arise if we pay closer attention to the Sabbath law of the Bible and particularly to the Sabbath ritual as it developed in the post-Biblical tradition.

Why is this social-hygienic law so important that it is placed among the Ten Commandments, which otherwise stipulate only the fundamental religious and ethical principles? Why is it explained with God's rest on the seventh day and what does this "rest" mean? Is God pictured in such anthropomorphic terms as to need a rest after six days of hard work? Why in the second version of the Ten Commandments is the Sabbath explained in terms of freedom rather than of God's rest? What is the common denominator of the two explanations? Moreover—and this is perhaps the most important question—how can we understand the intricacies of the Sabbath ritual in the light of the modern social-hygienic interpretation of rest? In the Old Testament, a man who "gathers sticks" (Num. 4:32 ff.) is considered a violator of the Sabbath law and punished by death. In the later development not only work in our modern sense is forbidden but activities like the following: making any kind of fire, even if it is for convenience's sake and does not require any physical effort; pulling a single grass blade or flower from the soil; carrying anything, even something as light as a handkerchief, on one's person. All this is not work in the sense of physical effort; its avoidance is often more of an inconvenience and discomfort than the doing of it would be. Are we dealing here with extravagant and compulsive exaggerations of an originally "sensible" ritual, or is our understanding of the ritual perhaps faulty and in need of revision?

A more detailed analysis of the symbolic meaning of the Sabbath ritual will show that we are dealing not with obsessional overstrictness but with a concept of work and rest which is different from our modern concept.

To begin with the essential point—the concept of work underlying the Biblical and the later Talmudic concept—is not simply that of physical effort but can be defined thus: *"Work" is any interference by man, be it constructive or destructive, with the physical world. "Rest" is a state of peace between man and nature*. Man must leave nature untouched, not change it in any way, neither by building nor by destroying anything; even the smallest change made by man in the natural process is a violation of "rest." The Sabbath is the day of peace between man and nature; work is any kind of disturbance of the man-nature equilibrium. On the basis of this general definition, we can understand the Sabbath ritual. Indeed, any heavy work like plowing or building is work in this as well as in our modern sense. But lighting a match and pulling up a grass blade, while not requiring effort, are symbols of human interference with the natural process, are a breach of peace between man and nature. On the basis of this principle, we understand also the Talmudic prohibition of carrying something of even little weight on one's person. In fact, the carrying of something as such is not forbidden. I can carry a heavy load within my house or my estate without violating the Sabbath ritual. But I must not carry even a handkerchief from one domain to the other, for instance, from the private domain of the house to the public domain of the street. This law is an extension of the idea of peace from the natural to the social realm. Just as man must not interfere with or change the natural equilibrium, he must refrain from changing the social order. That means not only not to do business but also the avoidance of that most primitive form of transference of property, namely, its local transference from one domain to the other.

The Sabbath symbolizes a state of complete harmony between man and nature and between man and man. By not working—that is to say, by not participating in the process of natural and social change—man is free from the chains of nature and from the chains of time, although only for one day a week.

The full significance of this idea can be understood only in the context of the Biblical philosophy of the relationship between man and nature. Before Adam's "fall"—that is, before man had reason—he lived in complete harmony with nature; the first act of disobedience, which is also the beginning of human freedom, "opens his eyes," he knows how to judge good and evil, he has become aware of himself and of his fellows, the same and yet unique, tied together by bonds of love and yet alone. Human history has begun. He is cursed by God for his disobedience. What is the curse? Enmity and struggle are proclaimed between man and animals ("And I will put enmity between thee [the serpent] and the woman, and between thy seed and her seed; it shall bruise thy head, and thou shalt bruise his heel"), between man and the soil ("cursed is the ground for thy sake; in sorrow shalt thou eat of it all the days of thy life; thorns also and thistles shall it bring forth to thee; and thou shalt eat the herb of the field; in the sweat of thy face shalt thou eat bread, till thou return unto the ground"), between man and woman ("and thy desire shall be to thy husband, and he shall rule over thee"), between woman and her own natural function ("in sorrow thou shalt bring forth children"). The original, pre-individualist harmony was replaced by conflict and struggle.[41]

What, then, is—in the prophetic view—the goal of man? To live in peace and harmony again with his fellow men, with animals, with the soil. The new harmony is different from that of paradise. It can be obtained only if man develops fully in order to become truly human, if he knows the truth and does justice, if

[41] Cf. E. Fromm, *Escape from Freedom* (New York: Rinehart & Co., 1941).

he develops his power of reason to a point which frees him from the bondage of man and from the bondage of irrational passions. The prophetic descriptions abound with symbols of this idea. The earth is unboundedly fruitful again, swords will be changed into plowshares, lion and lamb will live together in peace, there will be no war any more, women will bear children without pain (Talmudic), the whole of mankind will be united in truth and in love. This new harmony, the achievement of which is the goal of the historical process, is symbolized by the figure of the Messiah.

On this basis we can understand fully the meaning of the Sabbath ritual. The Sabbath is the anticipation of the Messianic time, just as the Messianic period is called the time of "continuous Sabbath." In fact, the Sabbath is not only the symbolic anticipation of the Messianic time but is considered its real precursor. As the Talmud puts it, "If all of Israel observed the Sabbath fully only once, the Messiah would be here."

Resting, not working, then, has a meaning different from the modern meaning of relaxation. In the state of rest, man anticipates the state of human freedom that will be fulfilled eventually. The relationship of man and nature and of man and man is one of harmony, of peace, of noninterference. Work is a symbol of conflict and disharmony; rest is an expression of dignity, peace and freedom.

In the light of this understanding some of the previously raised questions find an answer. The Sabbath ritual has such a central place in the Biblical religion because it is more than a "day of rest" in the modern sense; it is a symbol of salvation and freedom. This is also the meaning of God's rest; this rest is not necessary for God because he is tired, but it expresses the idea that great as creation is, greater and crowning creation is peace; God's work is a condescension; he must "rest," not because he is tired but because he is free and fully God only when he has ceased to work. So is man fully man only when he does not work, when he is at peace with nature and his fellow men; that is why the Sabbath commandment is at one time motivated by God's rest and at the other by the liberation from Egypt. Both mean the same and interpret each other: rest is freedom.

I would rather not leave this topic without referring briefly to some other aspects of the Sabbath ritual which are relevant to its full understanding.

The Sabbath seems to have been an old Babylonian holyday, celebrated every seventh day (Shapatu). But its meaning was quite different from that of the Biblical Sabbath. The Babylonian Shapatu was a day of mourning and self-castigation. It was a somber day, dedicated to the planet Saturn (our "Saturday" is still in its name devoted to Saturn, Saturn's-day) whose wrath one wanted to placate by self-castigation and self-punishment. Slowly the holyday changed its character. Even in the Old Testament it has lost the character of self-castigation and mourning; it is no longer an "evil" day, but a good day, destined for man's welfare. In the further development the Sabbath becomes more and more the very opposite of the sinister Shapatu. Sabbath becomes the day of joy and pleasure. Eating, drinking, singing, sexual intercourse, in addition to studying the Scriptures and later religious writings, have characterized the Jewish celebration of the Sabbath throughout the last two thousand years. From a day of submission to the evil powers of Saturn, Sabbath has become a day of freedom and joy. This change in mood and meaning can be fully understood only if we consider the meaning of Saturn. Saturn (in the old astrological and metaphysical tradition) symbolizes time. He is the god of time and hence the god of death. Inasmuch as man is like God, gifted with a soul, with reason, love and freedom, he is not subject to time or death. But inasmuch as man is an animal, with a body subject to the laws of nature, he is a slave to time and death. The Babylonians sought to appease the lord of time by self-castigation. The Bible in its Sabbath concept makes an entirely new attempt to solve the problem: by stopping interference with nature for one day you eliminate time; where there is no change, no work, no human interference there is no time. Instead of a Sabbath on which man bows down to the lord of time, the Biblical Sabbath symbolizes man's victory over time; time is suspended, Saturn is dethroned on his very day, Saturn's-day.

5. *Kafka's* The Trial

An outstanding example of a work of art written in symbolic language is Kafka's *The Trial*. As in so many dreams, events are presented, each of which is in itself concrete and realistic; yet the whole is impossible and fantastic. The novel, in order to be understood, must be read as if we listened to a dream—a long complicated dream in which external events happen in space and time, being representations of thoughts and feelings within the dreamer, in this case the novel's hero, K.

The novel begins with a somewhat startling sentence: "Someone must have been telling lies about Joseph K., for without having done anything wrong he was arrested one fine morning." [42]

K., we might say, begins the dream with an awareness that he is "arrested." What does "arrested" mean? It is an interesting word which has a double meaning. To be arrested can mean to be taken into custody by police officers and to be arrested can mean to be stopped in one's growth and development. An accused man is "arrested" by the police, and an organism is "arrested" in its normal development. The manifest story uses "arrested" in the former sense. Its symbolic meaning, however, is to be understood in the latter. K. has an awareness that he is arrested and blocked in his own development.

In a masterful little paragraph, Kafka explains why K. was arrested. This is how K. spent his life: "That spring K. had been accustomed to pass his evenings in this way: after work whenever possible—he was usually in his office until nine—he would take a short walk, alone or with some of his colleagues, and then go to a beer hall, where until eleven he sat at a table patronized mostly by elderly men. But there were exceptions to this routine, when, for instance, the Manager of the Bank, who highly valued his diligence and reliability, invited

[42] This and all subsequent quotations are from Franz Kafka, *The Trial*, (New York: Alfred A. Knopf, 1931).

him for a drive or for dinner at his villa. And once a week K. visited a girl called Elsa, who was on duty all night till early morning as a waitress in a cabaret and during the day received her visitors in bed."

It was an empty, routinized life, sterile, without love and without productiveness. Indeed, he was arrested, and he heard the voice of his conscience tell him of his arrest and of the danger that threatened his personality.

The second sentence tells us that "his landlady's cook, who always brought him his breakfast at eight o'clock, failed to appear on this occasion. That had never happened before." This detail seems unimportant. In fact, it is somewhat incongruous that after the startling news of his arrest such a trivial detail as his breakfast not having come should be mentioned; but, as in so many dreams, this seemingly insignificant detail contains important information about K.'s character. K. was a man with a "receptive orientation." All his strivings went in the direction of wanting to receive from others —never to give or to produce.[48]

He was dependent on others, who should feed him, take care of him, and protect him. He was still a child dependent on his mother—expecting everything from her help, using her and manipulating her. As is characteristic of people of this orientation, his main concern was to be pleasant and nice so that people, and in particular women, would give him what he needed; and his greatest fear was that people might become angry

[48] Cf. the description of the receptive orientation in E. Fromm, *Man for Himself* (New York: Rinehart & Co., 1947).

and withhold their gifts. The source of all good was believed to be outside, and the problem of living was to avoid the risk of losing the good graces of this source. The result is an absence of the feeling of his own strength and intense fear of being threatened with desertion by the person or persons whom he is dependent upon.

K. did not know who accused him or what he was accused of. He asked: "Who could these men be? What were they talking about? What authority could they represent?" A little later, when he talked with the "Inspector," a man higher up in the hierarchy of the court, the voice became somewhat more articulate. K. asked him all sorts of questions having nothing to do with the main question of what he was accused of, and in answering him the Inspector made a statement which contained one of the most important insights that could be given K. at that point—and for that matter to anyone who is troubled and seeks help. The Inspector said, "However, if I can't answer your questions, I can at least give you a piece of advice; think less about us and of what is to happen to you, think more about yourself instead." K. did not understand the Inspector's meaning. He did not see that the problem was within himself, that he was the only one who could save him, and the fact that he could not accept the Inspector's advice indicated his ultimate defeat.

This first scene of the story closes with another statement by the Inspector which throws a great deal of light on the nature of the accusation and of the arrest. "You'll be going to the Bank now, I suppose?" "To the Bank?" asked K. "I thought I was under arrest? . . . How can I go to the Bank, if I am under arrest?" "Ah, I see," said the Inspector, who had already reached the door. "You have misunderstood me. You are under arrest, certainly, but that need not hinder you from going about your business. You won't be hampered in carrying on the ordinary course of your life." "Then being arrested isn't so very bad," said K., going up to the Inspector. "I never suggested that it was," said the Inspector. "But in that case it would seem there was no particular necessity to tell me about it," said K., moving still closer."

Realistically, this could hardly happen. If a man is arrested, he is not permitted to continue his business life as usual nor in fact, as we see later, any of his other ordinary activities. This strange arrangement expressed symbolically that his business activities and everything else he did were of such a nature as not really to be touched by his arrest as a human being. Humanely speaking, he was almost dead, but he could continue his life as a bank official just the same, because this activity was completely separated from his existence as a human being.

K. had a vague awareness that he was wasting his life and rotting away fast. From here on, the whole novel deals with his reaction to this awareness and with the efforts he makes to defend and to save himself. The outcome was tragic; although he heard the voice of his conscience, he did not understand it. Instead of trying to understand the real reason for his arrest, he tended to escape from any such awareness. Instead of helping himself in the only way he could help himself—by recognizing the truth and trying to change—he sought help where it could not be found—on the outside, from others, from clever lawyers, from women whose "connections" he could use, always protesting his innocence and silencing the voice that told him he was guilty.

Perhaps he could have found a solution had it not been for the fact that his moral sense was confused. He knew only one kind of moral law: the strict authority whose basic commandment was "You must obey." He knew only the "authoritarian conscience," to which obedience is the greatest virtue and disobedience the greatest crime. He hardly knew that there was another kind of conscience—the humanistic conscience—which is our own voice calling us back to ourselves.[44]

In the novel, both kinds of conscience are represented symbolically: the humanistic conscience by the Inspector and later by the Priest; the authoritarian conscience by the court, the judges, the assistants, the crooked lawyers, and all others connected with the case. K's tragic mistake was that, although he heard the voice of his humanistic conscience, he mistook it for the voice of the authoritarian conscience and defended himself against the accusing authorities, partly by submission and partly by rebellion, when he should have fought for himself in the name of his humanistic conscience.

The "court" is described as despotic, corrupt and filthy; its procedure not based on reason or justice.

[44] Cf. the chapter on humanistic and authoritarian conscience in *Man for Himself, op. cit.*

The kind of lawbooks the judges used (shown him by the wife of an attendant) were a symbolic expression of this corruption. They were old dog-eared volumes, the cover of one was almost completely split down the middle, the two halves were held together by mere threads. "How dirty everything is here!" said K., shaking his head, and the woman had to wipe away the worst of the dust with her apron before K. would put out his hand to touch the books. He opened the first of them and found an indecent picture. A man and a woman were sitting naked on a sofa, the obscene intention of the draughtsman was evident enough, yet his skill was so small that nothing emerged from the picture save the all-too-solid figures of a man and a woman sitting rigidly upright and, because of the bad perspective, apparently finding the utmost difficulty even in turning toward each other. K. did not look at any of the other pages, but merely glanced at the title page of the second book. It was a novel entitled, *How Grete Was Plagued by Her Husband Hans*. "These are the lawbooks that are studied here," said K. "These are the men who are supposed to sit in judgment on me."

Another expression of the same corruption was that the attendant's wife was used sexually by one of the judges and one of the law students and that neither she nor her husband was permitted to protest. There is an element of rebelliousness in K.'s attitude toward the Court and a deep sympathy in the Law-Court Attendant who, after having given K. "a confidential look such as he had not yet ventured in spite of all his friendliness," said, "A man can't help being rebellious." But the rebelliousness alternated with submission. It never dawned upon K. that the moral law is not represented by the authoritarian court but by his own conscience.

To say that this idea never dawns upon him would not be quite correct. Once toward the end of his journey he came as close to the truth as he ever did. He heard the voice of his humanistic conscience represented by the priest in the Cathedral. He had gone to the Cathedral to meet a business acquaintance to whom he was to show the city, but this man had not kept the appointment and K. found himself alone in the Cathedral, a little forlorn and puzzled until suddenly an unambiguous and inescapable voice cried: "Joseph K.!"

K. started and stared at the ground before him. For the moment he was still free, he could continue on his way and vanish through one of the small dark wooden doors that faced him at no great distance. It would simply indicate that he had not understood the call, or that he had understood it and did not care. But if he were to turn round he would be caught, for that would amount to an admission that he had understood it very well, that he was really the person addressed, and that he was ready to obey. Had the priest called his name a second time K. would certainly have gone on, but since there was a persistent silence, though he stood waiting a long time, he could not help turning his head a little just to see what the priest was doing. The priest was standing calmly in the pulpit

as before, yet it was obvious that he had observed K.'s turn of the head. It would have
been like a childish game of hide-and-seek if
K. had not turned right round to face him.
He did so, and the priest beckoned him to
come nearer. Since there was now no need
for evasion, K. hurried back—he was both curious and eager to shorten the interview—with
long flying strides towards the pulpit. At the
first rows of seats he halted, but the priest
seemed to think the distance still too great,
he stretched out an arm and pointed with
sharply bent forefinger to a spot immediately
before the pulpit. K. followed this direction
too; when he stood on the spot indicated he
had to bend his head far back to see the priest
at all. "You are Joseph K.," said the priest,
lifting one hand from the balustrade in a
vague gesture. "Yes," said K., thinking how
frankly he used to give his name and what a
burden it had recently become to him; now-
adays people he had never seen before seemed
to know his name. How pleasant it was to
have to introduce oneself before being recognized! "You are an accused man," said the
priest in a very low voice. "Yes," said K. "So I
have been informed." "Then you are the
man I seek," said the priest. "I am the prison
chaplain." "Indeed," said K. "I had you sum-
moned here," said the priest, "to have a talk
with you." "I didn't know that," said K. "I
came here to show an Italian round the Cathedral." "A mere detail," said the priest. "What

is that in your hand? Is it a prayer-book?"
"No," replied K., "it is an album of sights
worth seeing in the town." "Lay it down," said
the priest. K. pitched it away so violently
that it flew open and slid some way along the
floor with dishevelled leaves. "Do you know
that your case is going badly?" asked the
priest. "I have that idea myself," said K. "I've
done what I could, but without any success so
far. Of course, my first petition hasn't been
presented yet." "How do you think it will
end?" asked the priest. "At first I thought it
must turn out well," said K., "but now I frequently have my doubts. I don't know how it
will end. Do you?" "No," said the priest, "but
I fear it will end badly. You are held to be
guilty. Your case will perhaps never get beyond a lower Court. Your guilt is supposed,
for the present, at least, to have been proved."
"But I am not guilty," said K.; "It's a misunderstanding. And, if it comes to that, how can
any man be called guilty? We are all simply
men here, one as much as the other." "That is
true," said the priest, "but that's how all
guilty men talk." "Are you prejudiced against
me too?" asked K. "I have no prejudices
against you," said the priest. "I thank you,"
said K.; "but all the others who are concerned in these proceedings are prejudiced
against me. They are influencing even out-
siders. My position is becoming more and
more difficult." "You are misinterpreting the

facts of the case," said the priest. "The verdict is not so suddenly arrived at, the proceedings only gradually merge into the verdict." "So that's how it is," said K., letting his head sink. "What is the next step you propose to take in the matter?" asked the priest. "I'm going to get more help," said K., looking up again to see how the priest took this statement. "There are several possibilities I haven't explored yet." "You cast about too much for outside help," said the priest disapprovingly, "especially from women. Don't you see that it isn't the right kind of help?" "In some cases, even in many, I could agree with you," said K., "but not always. Women have great influence. If I could move some women I know to join forces in working for me, I couldn't help winning through. Especially before this Court, which consists almost entirely of petticoat-hunters. Let the Examining Magistrate see a woman in the distance and he almost knocks down his desk and the defendant in his eagerness to get at her." The priest drooped over the balustrade, apparently feeling for the first time the oppressiveness of the canopy above his head. What could have happened to the weather outside? There was no longer even a murky daylight; black night had set in. All the stained glass in the great window could not illumine the darkness of the wall with one solitary glimmer of light. And at this very mo ment the verger began to put out the candles on the high altar, one after another. "Are you angry with me?" asked K. of the priest. "It may be that you don't know the nature of the Court you are serving." He got no answer. "These are only my personal experiences," said K. There was still no answer from above. "I wasn't trying to insult you," said K. And at that the priest shrieked from the pulpit! "Can't you see anything at all?" It was an angry cry, but at the same time sounded like the involuntary shriek of one who sees another fall and is startled out of himself.

The priest knew what the real accusation against K. was, and he also knew that his case would end badly. At this point K. had a chance to look into himself and to ask what the real accusation was, but, consistent with his previous orientation, he was interested only in finding out where he could get more help. When the priest said disapprovingly that he casts about too much for outside help, K.'s only response was fear that the priest was angry. Now the priest became really angry, but it was the anger of love felt by a man who saw another fall knowing he could help himself but could not be helped. There was not much more the priest could tell him. When K. moved in the direction of the doorway, the priest asked, "Do you want to leave already?" Although at that moment K. had not been thinking of leaving, he answered at once, "Of course, I must go. I'm the assistant manager of a Bank, they're waiting for me. I only came here to show a business friend from abroad round the Cathedral." "Well," said the priest, reaching out his hand to K., "then go." "But I can't find my way out alone in this darkness," said K.

K.'s was indeed the tragic dilemma of the person who could not find his way alone in the darkness and who insisted that only others could guide him. He sought help but he rejected the only help the priest could offer him. Out of his own dilemma he could not understand the priest. He asked, "Don't you want anything more to do with me?" "No," said the priest. "You were so friendly to me for a time," said K., "and explained so much to me, and now you let me go as if you cared nothing about me." "But you have to leave now," said the priest. "Well, yes," said K., "you must see that I can't help it." "You must first see that I can't help being what I am," said the priest. "You are the prison chaplain," said K. groping his way nearer to the priest again; his immediate return to the Bank was not so necessary as he had made out; he could quite well stay longer. "That means I belong to the Court," said the priest. "So why should I make any claims upon you? The Court makes no claims upon you. It receives you when you come, and it relinquishes you when you go."

The priest made it quite clear that his attitude was the opposite of authoritarianism. While he wanted to help K. out of love for his fellow men, he himself had no stake in the outcome of K.'s case. K.'s problem, in the priest's view, was entirely his own. If he refused to see he must remain blind—because no one sees the truth except by himself.

What is so confusing in the novel is the fact that it is never said that the moral law represented by the priest and the law represented by the court are different. On the contrary, in the manifest story the priest, being the prison chaplain, is part of the court system. But this confusion in the story symbolizes the confusion in K.'s own heart. To him the two are one, and just because he is not able to distinguish between them, he remains caught in the battle with the authoritarian conscience and cannot understand himself.

One year elapsed after K. had the first inkling of his arrest. It was now the evening before his thirty-first birthday and his case had been lost. Two men came to fetch him for the execution. In spite of his frantic efforts, he had failed to ask the right question. He had not found out what he was accused of, who accused him, and what was the way to save himself.

The story ends, as so many dreams do, in a violent nightmare. But while the executioners went through the grotesque formalities of preparing their knives, K. had for the first time an insight into his own problem. "I always wanted to snatch at the world with twenty hands, and not for a very laudable motive, either. That was wrong, and am I to show now that not even a whole year's struggling with my case has taught me anything? Am I to leave this world as a man who shies away from all conclusions? Are people to say of me after I am gone that at the beginning of my case I wanted it to finish, and at the end of it wanted it to begin again? I don't want that to be said."

For the first time K. was aware of his greediness and of the sterility of his life. For the first time he could see the possibility of friendship and human solidarity:

His glance fell on the top storey of the house adjoining the quarry. With a flicker as of a light going up, the casements of a window there suddenly flew open; a human figure, faint and insubstantial at that distance and that height, leaned abruptly far forward and stretched both arms still farther. Who was it? A friend? A good man? Someone who sympathized? Someone who wanted to help? Was it one person only? Or were they all there? Was help at hand? Were there some arguments in his favour that had been overlooked? Of course there must be. Logic is doubtless unshakeable, but it cannot withstand a man who wants to go on living. Where was the Judge whom he had never seen? Where was the High Court, to which he had never penetrated? He raised his hands and spread out all his fingers.

While all his life K. had been trying to find the answers, or rather to be given answers by others, at this moment he asked questions and the right questions. It was only the terror of dying that gave him the power to visualize the possibility of love and friendship and, paradoxically, at the moment of dying he had, for the first time, faith in life.